"Most leaders cast vision for an enterprise fully expecting to be the one who declares, 'Vision accomplished!' The leadership modeled by Jesus of Nazareth incorporated succession into its core: preparing 12 men to take the lead was essential to the explosive growth of the movement we call Christianity after His departure. In this book, Russ Crosson speaks into the vacuum of vision for the next generation!"

Bob Shank
Founder/CEO, The Master's Program

"My friend Russ Crosson is exactly right. Great leaders know intuitively that it's not about them, but about those they lead and the mission they steward. Easier said than done, right? That's why *What Makes a Leader Great* is such a timely book."

Andy Stanley
Senior Pastor, North Point Ministries

"In a society geared primarily on the self, Russ offers a refreshing perspective on being a servant leader. In Russ's book, you will find that being a great leader is not as glamorous as it seems, but rather a calling to humility."

Joel Manby
President/CEO Herschend Family Entertainment

"Great leaders empower others to reach their full potential! In doing so, productivity increases and the future leadership of the organization is in place for long lasting success. Russ Crosson shows you how!"

Coach Mark Richt
Head football coach, University of Georgia

"I wish every leader had the passion that Russ uses to build into young leaders. We all need to learn from his intentional practice and tips."

Jeff Shinabarger
Author, *More or Less: Choosing a Lifestyle of Excessive Generosity*

"From years of experience as a great leader himself, Russ offers a profound and different perspective on leadership. He merges the best practices of secular leadership with the 'why' of biblical principles as he leads us in the discovery of the one vital key to leadership success that is so often overlooked today."

Buck McCabe
Executive vice president, CFO,
Chick-fil-A, Inc.

"If the leader is the portrait of the desired destination then I can't think of a better person to write *What Makes a Leader Great*, than Russ Crosson... I have watched him engage, encourage and inspire younger leaders. He's been mentoring and shaping the next generation of leaders for years. That's why I'm so glad that he has put his passion on paper...This is a very important book that needs to be shared with others."

Dr. Crawford W. Loritts, Jr.
Senior pastor, Fellowship Bible Church,
author, speaker, radio host

"The greatest gift that current leaders can leave is a next generation of leaders who can take the organization to even greater heights. Russ's book encourages us to do so and provides valuable insights on how."

Bill Williams
CEO, The National Christian Foundation

"As a former NFL coach and currently the CEO of an international ministry, I can attest to the truths shared in this book. Great leadership is always about the people you mentor and then empower. This book will show you why great leadership is not about you but about those you lead. A great read."

Les Steckel
Veteran NFL coach and president/CEO
of the Fellowship of Christian Athletes

"Godly character. Brokenness. Humility. Endurance. These essential words you will discover in this remarkable book. It's a refreshing approach in what makes a great leader."

Karen Loritts
Conference speaker

WHAT MAKES
A LEADER
GREAT

RUSS CROSSON

HARVEST HOUSE PUBLISHERS
EUGENE, OREGON

Cover illustration © dmstudio / 123rf
Cover design by Dugan Design Group, Bloomington, Minnesota

Italics in quotations and Scripture verses indicate author's emphasis.

WHAT MAKES A LEADER GREAT
Copyright © 2014 Russell D. Crosson
Published by Harvest House Publishers
Eugene, Oregon 97402
www.harvesthousepublishers.com

Library of Congress Cataloging-in-Publication Data
    Crosson, Russ, 1953–
    What makes a leader great / Russ Crosson.
      pages cm
    ISBN 978-0-7369-6046-5 (hardcover)
    ISBN 978-0-7369-6047-2 (eBook)
    1. Leadership—Religious aspects—Christianity. 2. Management—Religious aspects—Christianity. 3. Business—Religious aspects—Christianity. I. Title.
    BV4597.53.L43C764 2014
    658.4'092—dc23

                      2014008734

Printed in China

15 16 17 18 19 20 21 22 / RDS-CD / 10 9 8 7 6 5 4 3 2

*To all leaders who aspire to leave
a mark that outlives themselves.*

Acknowledgments

This book would not have come to fruition without the encouragement and support of the folks at Harvest House Publishers. Bob Hawkins Jr., Terry Glaspey, Nick Harrison, and their capable team saw the vision for this content and worked tirelessly to make the final manuscript come together.

I owe a debt of gratitude to my partners at Ronald Blue & Co. for not only allowing me time to work on this project, but for also helping build a company that takes seriously the concepts shared herein. A special commendation to Patty Warren, my vice president of Human Resources, for leading the inculcation of these concepts into our organization and providing a detailed review of the content and the initial writing on several of the chapters. Angie Ramage was also a great help in developing the initial manuscript.

My long-time executive assistant, Bonnie Davidson, deserves special kudos. Not only did she keep the book on track by keeping the chapters in order, proofreading, and editing, but she did so while accomplishing with great aplomb the myriad of other tasks and projects I gave her. This book would not have been possible without her. Malissa Light and Scott Houser handled many administrative tasks such as gathering endorsements, working with the publisher on the cover, and other such details that made my life easier. Each of these folks assisted with excellence and professionalism for which I am grateful.

I am grateful to Julie, my wife of 34 years, who has been a constant source of encouragement for this book and to me in my role as CEO. I could not be an effective leader without her wise input and unwavering support and love. I've said I married above myself, and indeed I did!

Finally, I am grateful to my Lord and Savior, Jesus Christ, for lovingly and gently bringing me to the end of myself so I could be better used by Him. Without His work in my life this book would not have any content worth reading.

Contents

WHAT MAKES A LEADER *GREAT*

Empowering the Next Generation of Leaders

I t was an innocuous email from the managing director of our Seattle office that caught my eye. He was asking if I had time to spend a few minutes on the phone answering some questions from Bob Hawkins Jr., the president of Harvest House Publishers. I later found out his interest had been piqued when he heard how we were training our leaders at Ronald Blue & Co.

A couple of weeks later, my vice president of Human Resources, Patty Warren, and I spent about an hour on the telephone with Bob and his management team explaining our intentional approach to leadership development and how we were applying these principles to the next generation. Our involvement in the lives of our employees, especially regarding leadership training, was something we'd developed into a successful strategy over the past several years.

After talking for a few minutes, Bob said something I wasn't prepared to hear. He said, "Russ, I think you need to write a book on this subject. Many leaders and future leaders could benefit from what you and those at your company are doing."

I have to confess that my mind immediately raced to the myriad books on leadership I knew already existed, and I found myself discounting the idea. "Bob, we don't need another book on leadership," I countered. "Besides, I don't know if I have the time to devote to a project like that."

Bob allowed me to ramble for a moment before adding, "Russ, this could be a very important book for businesses like Ronald Blue & Co. and for people who sincerely want to learn what it means to pass on the right leadership traits to those coming behind them. If we don't pass the leadership baton well, the mission of whatever we're leading could be lost. It's all about passing on something of greater value to the next generation."

It was a sobering thought. Before I hung up the telephone that day, I agreed to consider what Bob was asking me to do. I realized we had touched on something much deeper than I first suspected. After several more discussions, I became convinced Bob was on to something. Writing a book on training the next generation of leaders *was* essential. After all, training leaders was a cornerstone of what we were doing at Ronald Blue & Co. And if what we were doing could help others prepare future leaders, this would be a worthwhile project.

Each one of us is a leader. Each one of us has something to pass on to others. You certainly don't have to be an executive in an office setting to bear the title of "leader." At some point, all of us will have opportunities to make decisions that can potentially change the course of a situation or the life of another person. Men and women from all walks of life are asked to lead, but few have the tools or the motivation needed to teach others to do the same.

I realize there are countless books on leadership in the marketplace, but most are on subjects like "How to lead" or "What a leader should do." There seems to be very few books on *why* we lead:

- Why are you in a position of leadership?
- Why are you leading your family, business, church group, parachurch organization, or other worth-while endeavor?
- Why do we need leadership?
- Why is leadership important?

The more I thought about seeing a book on this subject come together, the more excited I became—especially when I thought about unpacking the *why* of leadership. When we answer the *why* question, we're choosing to look beyond ourselves to a greater cause. We're opening the door to a new purpose and to helping others in their quest to reach their full potential. Basically, the *why* explains the reason for our existence. The *why* is what makes it important to get out of bed every morning. In the end, I believe you'll see that the answer to this *why* question is the reason your life matters.

In a nutshell, I ask you to consider this explanation of *why*:

We lead in order to replace ourselves.

To some, this explanation may seem trite and simple. To others, it may seem somewhat intimidating. However, at the end of the day we're not successful leaders unless we have successors. If we don't replace ourselves, whatever we're leading will end when we retire or die.

French President Charles de Gaulle said, "Our graveyards are full of *indispensable* men." He was talking about men and women who falsely believed they could *not* be replaced; therefore, there was no forethought about the next generation. I want to challenge any leader today who hasn't considered the devastating effects of his or her sudden departure to do so.

Over these past few years, we've witnessed the death of many important Christian leaders. Each time I've wondered what type of succession plan that leader had in place so the vision God had given him or her would continue. What will it mean to your company, ministry, and family if you are suddenly gone? The most effective leaders in the future will be those who realize their mission is not about them but about those who come after them. These leaders realize they *are* dispensable, so they plan ahead by training those who will one day take their place.

I'm a former math teacher, so I know that exponential power is much greater than addition or multiplication. The ultimate output of the man or woman who is focused on future leaders is exponential as generation after generation gets impacted. The end result of a leader willing to focus on the future is far greater than the leader who is only looking to be a great leader while he or she is at the helm. Your family, business, ministry, church, or whatever you are leading will be much stronger today and in the future if your focus includes shaping the lives of others coming up behind you. They will be the ones to keep your vision and mission alive.

My hope is that the simple concepts in this book will become a pathway of new thinking for you. I pray they will impact your life as they have mine as I continue to lead Ronald Blue & Co. and my family. May these thoughts empower you to be a great leader today and a great leader of the future.

Russ Crosson

THE LEADER

1

Off the Farm

Early Thoughts on Leadership

Acool breeze was blowing through the trees, and fall was definitely in full swing in the leafy suburb of Kansas City that we called home. Recently fallen leaves had swirled under our feet as Julie and I loaded the last few items into our cars and the U-Haul truck. Julie would drive one car, and I would drive the U-Haul pulling the other car. All of our belongings were in these three vehicles.

We'd been married slightly over a year. A few months earlier, I'd quit my job as a high school math teacher and coach to take a job with a start-up financial-planning company in Atlanta, Georgia. I'd never been east of the Mississippi River, but I figured at age twenty-seven it was time to take a leap of faith and go for it. After all, financial planning seemed to be a good vocation, and I would still be able to use my math skills. Plus I'd often been told I was good with people, so this seemed to be a good fit.

As we settled into the two-day drive down the interstate headed east, I couldn't help but daydream about what might be in store. Would this job afford me an opportunity to "run something" like I'd been able to do by coaching the sophomore basketball team? Would I one day be able to be in charge of the company? Would I become the boss or one of the leaders? I didn't realize it at the time, but questions and dreams like these revealed my limited vision of leadership. Little did I know that the *process* to becoming a leader and someone who learned to think beyond himself would take years and many difficult moments to develop.

Life on the Farm

As the miles rolled by, I became reflective. I realized almost immediately that Kansas and the life I had there was becoming a distant speck in the rearview mirror. I grew up on a wheat farm in north-central Kansas and attended a one-room country school. You know, a "little house on the prairie"-type school complete with an outhouse. It held eight grades, and I attended there until sixth grade. The school year was eight months long so we farm kids could help with chores, harvest the crops, and work around the farm as needed.

I'm the eldest of five children, and we didn't have much in the way of material possessions. But we did have love and all that we needed. Mom made all my clothes until I was in ninth grade. We grew most of our food, and I guess you could say we were organic farmers even before that became trendy. We had range-fed chickens, range-fed beef, garden vegetables, and milk straight from the cow. (Yes, we drank unpasteurized milk. Today, I know people who drive miles to get that kind of milk.) We had food, shelter, and clothing, but not much beyond those things. I knew there was a big world out there, but for the most part I was content in my little world on our farm.

Though my childhood was a hand-to-mouth existence, it

was critical to my upbringing and development. It taught me an incredible work ethic—something I still have. I can easily recall what it felt like to get up early and see the sun come up over the fields as I headed out to the barn to feed our livestock. Dad always told me, "Son, if you don't feed the livestock, no one else will feed them. How would you like to not be fed?" I obviously liked to eat, so early morning chores, late-night chores, and long days in the field were just part of growing up. It was simply what we did. Even today that life is still a reminder to me that we're placed here to be caretakers of God's creation. Dad was right! If I didn't do what I was given to do, who would do it?

Learning Confidence and Independence

I recognized early on that I couldn't do everything, but I could do what Dad had given me to do. And I learned I could do it well. Work on the farm gave me confidence that I could do things on my own and make good decisions. Independence was fostered at an early age. I was put on a tractor at age twelve and was driving a large combine by age fourteen. Driving pickups and cars on the country roads at an early age was a given. From the last day of school in June until we started up again in the fall, I was on the farm working from sunup till sundown.

When I was six years old, I suffered a significant fall that exacerbated a condition called Legg-Perthes disease, which causes a softening of the heads on femur bones. For four years, I was on crutches and had to wear leg braces. One entire summer was spent in bed with a cast covering both legs. The doctors thought this might help force the femurs back into place.

When the casts came off, my leg muscles were atrophied,

so participating in most sports was out of the question. However, after much badgering and complaining on my part, the doctors and my parents finally relented. With a lot of work getting my muscles in shape, I was able to play basketball during my freshman year in high school. I'd spent countless hours shooting balls at an old hoop next to our chicken house on the farm, so when I finally got a chance to play on a team I did well. Eventually, I received college scholarship offers. With each one I became more prideful. My success on the basketball court reinforced my developing mindset that the best leaders were those who got the job done. I became the leader of our basketball team because I was the best player. Performance equaled success. At that point, it was all "me vs. my teammates."

During this time, I also achieved great success in 4-H. I was president of our local club and owned an award-winning flock of sheep. I also won an all-expense-paid trip to Chicago where I got to shake hands with then President Nixon. That success, along with my basketball prowess and independent spirit, fed my belief that if a person worked hard enough, he or she could succeed. Success and leadership were tied to a person's abilities and work ethic. I had no clue that God had a different perspective.

I went on to graduate *summa cum laude* from college and accepted my first teaching job at a large high school in a suburb of Kansas City. I was thrilled when they allowed me to coach the sophomore basketball team. "This is *my* team!" I assured myself. I was in charge. I didn't have to report to anyone. I was in control so I could build the team how I desired. I was "the boss," as my mom would so proudly say. I'd learned growing up that it was good to be the boss, to be the one who told people what to do. That was what the Crossons were good at—being bosses.

But now all that was behind me. Julie and I were driving toward Atlanta and a new business opportunity. The miles flew by as my thoughts drifted to what lay ahead. I wondered how long it would be before I would be in charge, before I would become the boss. I knew my long-term career perspective included wanting to run something. I didn't just want to work for someone; I wanted to be the one in charge. I wanted others to work for me. Little did I know that I was about to face a very painful learning experience. Thankfully it became one that helped define for me the *true* characteristics of *great* leaders.

My Early Days at Ronald Blue & Co.

Ron Blue had started his company a few months before my arrival. I was the second professional he hired for his fledgling enterprise. As I mentioned, I believed my background in math coupled with my ability to connect and communicate with people would guarantee success in the career field of financial planning. Was I in for a surprise.

I knew my way around a math classroom and a basketball court, but what I found in Atlanta was a total change from coaching and teaching. In this new arena, I was totally in the dark. Even though financial planning was a relatively new industry back then, Ron was a CPA so his tax expertise and financial acumen allowed him to move seamlessly into this new environment. He was quite comfortable operating on the same playing field as the bankers, accountants, brokers, and life-insurance professionals who, up until that time, had been the primary sources of financial advice and investment products for people desiring guidance.

Three weeks after my arrival, Ron's next professional hire was another CPA. That left me feeling outnumbered and intimidated. The CPAs and other professionals (an estate attorney shared office space with us) would sit around the office discussing trusts, tax-planning strategies, and the like, while I sat there totally clueless. They might as well have been speaking a foreign language. My self-confidence was shaken to the core. How could I reach my goal to lead the company and be in charge when I didn't know anything about this business?

I did the only thing I knew to do, and that was to buckle down and learn all there was to know about financial planning. I studied taxes, financial statements, insurance products, investments, estate planning, wills, trusts, and more. I spent a great number of Saturdays learning to use a 10-key calculator and getting my speed up by practicing adding up phone numbers from the phone book. The ability to crank out numbers with the 10-key was critical to doing financial planning in those precomputer days.

Because of tax law changes, I soon found I was up-to-speed with my colleagues because everything was changing for them too. I was once again on a more level playing field. As those early years went by, my competitive nature was hard at work. I reasoned that if I became highly productive and brought in new clients, Ron would notice and my advancement to a position of leadership would be guaranteed. After all, that had been my experience thus far in life. Work hard and produce and you get ahead, eventually becoming the leader.

The Promotion

Then it happened! In 1986, Ron promoted me to Chief Operating Officer (COO), which made me the No. 2 guy in the company. At age 33 I was right where I thought I would be. I was *in charge*. Everyone reported to me, and I reported to Ron. I liked being out front. I believed this is what leaders did—they got out front and told everyone what to do, where to go, and how to follow. This had been my life experience in basketball and 4-H, and it was still working perfectly. The same thing was happening in the business world. I was *the* man—*the* leader.

The next six years were good. A downturn in the economy in 1988 and 89 was followed by three great years, culminating in 1992 being our best year up to that point. Well, the best year for the firm. It would become the worst year for me personally.

The Demotion

I'll never forget where I was on that August day in 1993 when reality hit. Eight months earlier Ron had told me he was going to name a new COO. Though I was frustrated, I rationalized his decision away. I chose to believe the change wasn't due to anything I'd done or hadn't done. It was simply an opportunity to put an older gentleman who had joined us from a similar company in the position. He had more experience, so it made sense.

But the call I received on that August day changed my thinking. I was sitting in a partner's office in our Atlanta location when the call came in. The new COO was on the other end of the line. He calmly told me my income was going to be reduced by 40 percent. He also told me if I wanted to stay with the company, I would be put in charge of corporate training. I felt a knot in my stomach. A few months earlier, everyone in the firm was reporting to me. Now I was being offered a position with only four people to manage! My head was spinning as I struggled to understand what I'd just heard.

How could this be happening? I asked repeatedly. *Hadn't I proven myself over and over? Surely my production demonstrated that I was a great leader. Weren't results what leading the company was about? Hadn't we just had our best year ever under my watch?* The struggle going on inside of me was tremendous. That night as I sat at our kitchen table still stunned, I tried to explain to Julie what had happened. I had trouble comprehending it myself. How did I go from being the No. 2 guy to almost being out of the firm? I spent the next several days trying to understand what went wrong. I wanted to know what I'd done to end up in this position, but I couldn't figure it out.

I'm sure many people have gone through a similar situation. Countless individuals have received news like this or worse. The shock was so great that I couldn't eat or sleep. I wrestled with God for answers. Finally, after a couple weeks, I came to the end of myself. I was humbled. It was as if all the wind went out of my sails. I was driven to my knees. I quit fighting. I quit trying to figure my circumstances out. I quit searching for the answer that would make sense of what had happened. I finally decided, "It was what it was," and God had me in this crucible for a reason.

What I Eventually Discovered

I may have done a good job producing great results, but apparently there was more to being a leader than I realized. It became clear to me that I had made a lot of mistakes over the prior six years. I had communicated to those reporting to me that it was "my way or the highway." The truth is, I was poor in relationship management. I had lost the trust of those I was leading because they didn't feel I cared about them. I murmured behind people's backs. I came across as intolerant of anyone who didn't do things my way. The bottom line was that I was prideful. And it was becoming quite clear that what I *thought* was leadership wasn't really leadership at all.

I took some solace in the fact that I was not the first 40-year-old to go through a wilderness experience. Being relegated to manager of our training program felt like I was out in the middle of nowhere. Moses had a similar experience. We all know the story. He realized he was one of God's people. He saw the suffering the Israelites were facing, and because he had an incredible "can-do attitude," he decided to rescue the entire nation by beginning with murder. He wanted to save God's people from the hands of the Egyptians. He probably had God's desire within his heart even before the Lord called to him, but the timing wasn't right. His motivation was self-centered, and the method he chose was infinitely flawed. Moses' way was not God's way. As a result of his self-effort, Moses spent many years in a foreign country and, later, 40 years in the wilderness being tested, tried, and humbled by God.

He could have resisted—pushed back and refused to submit to God's training. But we can surmise that each day his life became more in step with God's will. He may have been demoted, but he had not been forgotten. He may have once been a prince in Pharaoh's household, but he was to become a shepherd of God's flock.

The culmination of Moses' experiences and growth in Midian came down to one moment: the time he knelt before the burning bush. The sandals came off, and he bowed his face before the Lord (Exodus 3). He was finally prepared and equipped to lead God's people out of Egypt.

We are all in the process of being prepared by God before we can lead others. In the introduction to this book, I wrote, "At some point, all of us will have opportunities to make decisions that can potentially change the course of a situation or the life of another person. Men and women from all walks of life are asked to lead." God has a plan for your life, and He wants to equip you to make an eternal impact on the generation coming up behind you. Moses' life touched an entire nation. But before that could take place, he had to surrender emotionally and mentally to the Lord so that he could be used effectively.

I began to realize that, like Moses, I was in God's classroom, and He had my full attention. I had a choice: I could leave the firm angry or I could stay and let God prepare me for what He had for me in the future. I chose to stay. I believed I could continue to produce while learning what I needed to learn. After I learned what I needed to learn, I knew I'd be free to leave the company and do something else.

Called to Be Chief Executive Officer

Little did I know that by the time I was through the ten-year learning process, the board of directors of Ronald Blue & Co. would ask me to take over as chief executive officer (CEO) when Ron retired. I thought I was ready to run the firm in 1986, but I was dead wrong. Only after pride had been rooted out and replaced by humility could I truly lead.

I will write more about this later, but I'm convinced that the best leaders are those who have been humbled along the way. Only after a person has been hurt deeply and surrendered his or her will to God is he or she equipped to lead. No matter how talented, gifted, or charismatic the person may be, he or she can't be a "future generation leader" until the lesson is learned that leading isn't about him- or herself. This is what countless people from every walk of life have had to learn, myself included. The flawed ideas I learned on the farm about being the boss, being in charge, and being independent had to be rooted out for me to learn how to truly lead with the right motives.

How about you? Do you have the mistaken idea that leadership is all about you? Hopefully, the next chapter will convince you otherwise.

2

OUT OF THE DIRT

It's Not About You

While reading through the Old Testament, I gained a deeper understanding of a very simple truth: *People who find themselves in leadership roles have been placed there by God and not by themselves.* Moses didn't sign up to lead the Israelite captives out of Egypt. Joseph, Jacob's son, had no idea that being sold into captivity by his brothers would enable him to save his people during a famine many years later. Jesus was probably the only One who fully knew the depth of His commission and call. He understood the reality of what it meant to be a leader. Most of us don't, and that is why God has to spend time—years for some—training and molding us before we're able to assume the leadership responsibilities He has for us.

I was reminded of an important truth as I read these words spoken by Jehu to Baasha, the leader of Israel: "Then the word of the LORD came to Jehu…concerning Baasha: 'I lifted you up from the dust and appointed you [leader] over my people Israel'" (1 Kings 16:1-2). The Lord reminded me that I too was made from dust, and yet He had given my life purpose. This Scripture really hit home and brought a new perspective on the subject of leadership. We are made from dust, and yet God works in and through us to accomplish great things. Unless we grasp this concept, we will never understand the full depth of the leadership role God is calling us to fulfill.

We often think leadership is glamorous, but it's not. It is a call to *humility*, especially when we reflect on the fact that the only reason we're in positions of leadership is because of God's goodness, grace, and providential appointment. Being a leader should motivate us to draw nearer to the Lord and to learn what He wants to teach us.

Dirt, from which we are made, is not a bad thing. It's a point of beginning. Realizing we are from dirt can lead us to a place where we understand our limitations and our need for God's strength, wisdom, patience, and courage. It can also open us up to the fact that we are not as valuable as we think. My role as a leader doesn't just entail climbing a corporate ladder. In fact, as in the cases of Moses and Joseph, it almost looks like our lives often take an opposite turn.

Leadership means learning to consider those under us more than we consider ourselves. Far too often, people accept positions simply because they want to build their résumés, but God isn't interested in building résumés! He wants to build a band of followers who have His character locked tightly within their hearts, minds, and lives.

Humble Leadership

If you're in a leadership role, one of the first things you must learn is this: *It is not your moxie that got you there.* Remember: You are dirt. God placed you in your position for a purpose.

Years after my rise and subsequent fall from leadership at Ronald Blue & Co., someone asked me what I'd learned during that time. To be honest, my answer wasn't "endurance" or "how to gather a sense of greater strength within me." I had plenty of both of those. From earlier life experiences, I knew about focus, self-control, discipline, and overcoming obstacles. I also knew how to succeed in life on a material level. But those experiences couldn't teach me the one thing I needed the most—how to have a humble spirit before God. The rough course I had to follow to take in that lesson taught me an unforgettable principle: *My life, my job, and my career were not about me.* My life was about *fulfilling the mission God had given me.* To do that, I had to humble myself before Him.

Humility is a choice. Moses spent years learning this principle. Joseph was banished to prison to learn it. Even David, the anointed king of Israel, was forced to run for his life from a deranged king who was bent on destroying him. In these times—these wilderness experiences—they learned the deeper lessons of God. They learned to listen and rest in humility—the one character quality we all need the most.

The apostle Peter was a rough and decisive fisherman. I'm sure he knew the waters of the Sea of Galilee like the back of his hand, but that personal knowledge wasn't enough to equip him to be a leader. He had to learn humility. Peter later wrote:

> Be shepherds of God's flock that is under your care,
> watching over them—not because you must, but
> because you are willing, as God wants you to be;
> not pursuing dishonest gain, but eager to serve;
> not lording it over those entrusted to you, but

being examples to the flock...Clothe yourselves
with humility toward one another, because, "God
opposes the proud but shows favor to the humble."
Humble yourselves, therefore, under God's mighty
hand, that he may lift you up in due time (1 Peter
5:2-3,5-6).

Oswald Chambers, one of the most widely read devotional
writers and a man who has impacted generation after generation with his call to live a surrendered life as a follower of Christ,
wrote,

As we respond to the call of God, He gives us a
vision of what He would have us be and do for Him,
but there is often a valley to go through before the
vision is brought down to earth. Like Moses, we
may need to go through a period of wilderness
discipline before we can lead God's people forth.
Both self-confidence and self-despising must be
dealt with.[1]

At some point each one of us will come to a place where we
must make a decision: humble ourselves and become a leader
God can use or go in our own determination, strength, and
pride and never be all we can be as leaders.

Death Must Come to Our Egos

I vividly remember the day I quit fighting and decided to
submit to the leadership of the person who was now over me.
I knew I was at a dangerous point. If I chose to continue along
my prideful path, there would be serious consequences. I had

come to a breaking point. This is when I finally realized that life was not about me. It was about living for something and Someone much greater than anything I could do or envision on my own. My ego had finally been rooted out. I had come to the point where I acknowledged that God was my source of security and self-worth. He was my only audience and authority, the only One worthy of my praise.

When leaders focus on themselves and not the mission, it can be a short step to capitulation and compromise. Why? Because focusing on the leader instead of the mission allows people's egos to take over. Ego can be viewed as an acronym for "Edging God Out." When that happens, pride, fear, self-promotion, and protection take over. Focus is on self instead of God.

If a person is to be a great leader, he or she needs to be careful to recognize that the growth of ego can be the first step toward decline. Jim Collins, in his book *How the Mighty Fall*, builds a compelling case that the first step to the decline of an organization is hubris born of success. An entity has success, and hubris (defined as excessive pride) sets in among the leadership and decline is imminent.[2]

Growth of ego can be a difficult thing for any leader to deal with because leaders are typically talented in many areas, quite skilled, and usually charismatic. These are the very things that attract people to them. People who are attracted to leaders like this usually applaud the leaders and, in some cases, even worship them, telling them how great they are. If leaders begin to believe their own press instead of holding fast to the fact they've been appointed to their roles by God, they'll quickly find themselves on a very slippery slope.

In *The Enemies of Excellence*, Greg Salciccioli writes,

> When we focus on our egos, we tend to think in all-or-nothing terms—"either I achieve this one goal or I lose everything." But excellence does not work this way. When we decide to do what's right, regardless of the outcome, we will always discover greater opportunity...The "something" of greater value is a higher achievement than self-advancement. This is the great foresight of altruists. They clearly see the right choice and invest their time, talents, and treasures accordingly. They don't just live for the now, but for the future and the betterment of themselves and mankind. They understand the welfare and wealth of lifting up a fellow human being. But the person who struggles with ego only thinks of himself or herself. That person rarely considers others and how leadership decisions will affect them.[3]

Scott Rodin, president of Rodin Consulting of Spokane, Washington, and former president of Eastern Baptist Theological Seminary, summarized much of what I was experiencing during my time of transformation:

> At the very heart of my reflection on my service lies this major conclusion...I was wrong. I was wrong in my understanding and preconceived notions of leadership...I was wrong in my expectations of others and myself. And I was wrong in my motivations, which may be the hardest thing to admit...

I have come to believe that true Christian leadership is an ongoing, disciplined practice of becoming a person of no reputation, and thus, becoming more like Christ in this unique way. In his reflections on Christian leadership, Henri Nouwen refers to this as resisting the temptation to be relevant. He says, "I am deeply convinced that the Christian leader of the future is called to be completely irrelevant and to stand in this world with nothing to offer but his or her own vulnerable self."[4]

The Mission Is Bigger Than the Leader

Due to ego and self-sufficiency, very few leaders actually lead with the idea of training others to take their places one day. They mistakenly lead as if they will continue in their leadership position for years to come. This was true of me. I led because I knew I was good at it. I had the answers, ability, and energy. But I had to be brought down in order to understand that the vision and mission of Ronald Blue & Co. were bigger than me personally.

Most leaders lead because they believe they are meant to lead, called to lead, and destined to lead—but not necessarily because they see a responsibility to train the men and women who will come after them. I believe today's leaders must begin to think differently. They have to face the fact they're not going to be with their company, ministry, or firm until eternity. If they don't understand this, when they either leave or die their companies, ministries, or firms will die with them.

Most people (staff and clients) want to be involved in

something that will have eternal purpose. They are attracted to something bigger than themselves. While they may be impressed with you as a leader, what really inspires them is what is at the core of the entity or organization. They want to be part of something that motivates them to get out of bed every morning and have an impact on this world. They are compelled by the *why* of the organization, and not as much by the *what* or *how* of a company.

Simon Sinek, in his influential work on the power of *why*, points this out quite clearly. When the leader explains why they do what they do, there is meaning and a reason to buy into the vision:

> Asking *why* is important because it aligns our hearts with God's. It moves us toward Him and fulfilling His commission. It also motivates us toward meaningful work. It keeps us from drifting because we are focused on something much greater than ourselves. Discovering why we are here keeps us from being commoditized. It is a key to growth and helps us build strong enduring relationships.[5]

At Ronald Blue & Co., answering the *why* question helps our clients reap the rewards of their willingness to invest and give to others. We have a very clearly articulated mission: *We exist to help Christians become financially free to assist in fulfilling the Great Commission*. We provide financial, estate, tax, investment, and philanthropic counsel to help folks have "peace of mind" in their financial lives. Our staff and clients are attracted to this mission, which is bigger than they are. They like the idea of impacting this world through giving.

Ron started the company many years ago, and it is my job as the current CEO to ensure that this mission stays alive and well. He successfully transferred the fire of this mission to me, and now it is my responsibility to make sure it continues by keeping the fire burning within the leader or leaders who will succeed me. That's true of any entity or organization. As we are learning, this requires intentional focus on those who will lead in the future. It also demands that we never forget the mission, the brand, and the reason for our existence. We must not think even for a moment that it's about us. We're simply stewards of our firms, ministries, and organizations for a period of time.

This type of thinking also applies to the family structure. As the leader of his family, the dad may think it's all about him—but it's not. It's not about his knowledge, skills, abilities, or decision-making capability as husband and dad. If at any time he places more emphasis on his skills as a dad and doesn't make the switch to realizing the most important factor is his loved ones, then his family is at risk. American author and critic Neil Postman noted, "Children are the living messages we send to a time that we will not see."[6] After we're gone, the most powerful mark we leave behind is the one carried on through the lives and testimonies of those we loved and led. As a father, my focus is on transferring the things I've learned to my children.

The Crosson family mission statement is: *"Create an environment and maximize opportunities to enhance the development of a godly posterity."* (*Posterity* in this context is our children.) When Julie and I wrote this statement, we realized it was bigger than either of us. It states very clearly that we are living to *leave a legacy*. For the Crosson name to live on into future generations with the same values it carries today, we must make intentional decisions for the future. Where we live, how we spend money, and what we do with our free time are impacted by this statement. I realize that as the father it is my job to implement Psalm 78:4-7:

> We will not conceal them from their children, but tell to the generation to come the praises of the LORD, and His strength and His wondrous works that He has done. For He established a testimony in Jacob and appointed a law in Israel, which He commanded our fathers that they should teach them to their children, that the generation to come might know, even the children yet to be born, that they may arise and tell them to their children, that they should put their confidence in God and not forget the works of God, but keep His commandments (NASB).

This passage isn't about me as the leader of my family; rather, it's about the generations to come after me. It speaks to my role as a father and a generational leader who must stay true to the mission of God, teach His truths so the next generation will know them, and maintain an ongoing desire to know Him personally.

Build *Followers* Not Fans

In addition to the importance of eliminating ego, another challenge for a charismatic leader who has great talent is how to handle *fans* vs. *followers*. Fans are people who are excited or stirred to action. They may be inspired by the leader, but they never move to the position of followers. Fans are enthusiastic and challenged by the leader's vision, but they have not made the switch to being supporters and advocates of the mission. The fire isn't burning deeply within them, and their dedication to the mission is at a superficial level.

Followers, by definition, are people who come behind the leader and choose to be led by the leader. These people are pursuing, chasing, and moving in the same direction as the leader toward something bigger than all of them. True followers are disciples, adherents, and imitators—not of the leader, but of the mission. They are "next in line" in the pursuit of the mission of the entity or organization. They are in step with the leader and "going with" him or her, which implies the followers are seeking what the leader is. Fans only follow the leader; followers follow the mission.

Jesus had both. He had fans—those people who hung on His every word and wanted to be close to Him to be healed. They fell away when times got tough. He also had followers—His disciples and some others. Jesus was totally absorbed by the mission His Father had given Him. He knew He came to die and do the will of the Father. His disciples and the others came to appreciate this great mission (saving the world from sin) and became *followers*. This is the power of a compelling mission. The mission attracts followers. These followers surrendered their lives to make sure the message of salvation carried on. They also came to discover that through the power of the Holy Spirit they could continue to do great things just as

Jesus had done (John 14:12). Great leaders know this is the case. They experience it. Since the mission is not about them personally and they're investing in those who come after them, they will be thrilled when their followers carry on.

What started me thinking about this concept of "Fan vs. Follower" was a statement by a friend who asked me if I thought a certain leader of a well-known church was irreplaceable. I contend that the specific role a person plays in a business, church, and/or family could be irreplaceable. However, if he or she is really a *leader* with followers and not just fans, they will be replaceable in their leadership role within the entity. As a result, the mission, brand, and reason for the entity will be preserved and carried on without that specific leader. For example, Truett Cathy, who founded Chick-fil-A, is irreplaceable in his specific roles (founder, visionary, entrepreneur, spokesman, and so forth). However, he is also a leader who has thought through the future and has prepared a team of men and women to carry on the mission of the company after he is no longer the leader. He has stepped aside as CEO to let his son (after years of training him) take over. By doing so, he ensured the company will continue on.

Another example is my company. Ron, in his role as founder and visionary of Ronald Blue & Co., can't be replaced. However, by his training me and, subsequently, the myriad of other financial advisors in our company, he is no longer the sole person providing financial advisory services to clients. As a result, the mission of the company continues even now although Ron is no longer active in the day-to-day business.

A great orator of a large church may not be able to be

replaced by a similarly skilled individual. But if the leader has really led the church in the right way, the mission will carry on when he is no longer in his role. A great CEO will make sure the company is in good hands and continues undeterred when he or she will no longer be in an active role. To make sure the mission continues, it's incumbent that we realize leadership is not about you or me. It's about those who are following us. To understand this principle well, we have to come to the conclusion that we were created from dirt and dust, and we have only been given a short amount of time on this earth to make our lives count. We must realize we're simply caretakers and stewards of the entities we're leading—church, family, ministry, business—during our limited time on the "stage of action." The real question? How will we impact the lives of those around us in a positive way and encourage the people who make up the next generation to follow our goals and mission?

A good measurement of whether someone is really a great leader or just a great contributor to an entity is what happens after the leader is gone. Does the mission carry on or does it die? If the entity doesn't carry on, then that person wasn't a great leader in the biblical sense. He or she was simply someone who was very good at what he or she did. They had fans, not followers.

Conclusion

As I did in my earlier years, you too may accomplish a great deal—garnering awards, accolades, ribbons, and so forth. But the end result of your leadership won't be measured by your personal successes. Rather, your success as a leader will be measured by those who come after you. Do they continue to fuel the original passion of the mission so nothing is lost? Whatever you're leading should continue long after you're gone. If it doesn't, the question could be asked, "Did you really ever lead?"

The ministry of Christ continues today not only because of Jesus' substitutionary death on the cross and the sending of the Holy Spirit, but also because Jesus invested His life in others. His work with the disciples is being replicated each and every day. Will your work continue? This is the true measure of leadership. A true leader is not successful unless he or she has a successor. Great leaders have followers.

At this point you may be thinking, *If leading isn't about me, why do I exist? Why am I in this leadership position?* We'll unpack that in the next chapter.

3

WHY ME?

Your Reason for Existence

If being a leader isn't about you, then why do you exist, and why are you in a leadership position? Have you stopped to wonder why you do what you do each day? Seriously. Why do you get out of bed? Why does it matter that you exist? Does anyone care? Do you get up and do what's necessary to just receive a paycheck? Or is there something bigger happening?

Let's look at the life Jesus led to gain some insights into this "why" question. He was, without a doubt, the greatest leader who ever lived. He understood what God had given Him to do. His mission was to die on the cross for the sins of mankind. As He fulfilled this mission, He inspired and challenged a ragtag group of men to engage with Him in the goal of changing the world. They became His disciples, His followers. At His core, Jesus was a *disciple maker*. As a disciple maker, He modeled two characteristics that answer the "why we exist" question and should be evidenced in our lives as leaders.

First, Jesus' passion for His mission was unparalleled and uncompromised. Second, He lived a life of sacrifice to accomplish His mission. In fact, paying the ultimate price by giving His very life *was* His primary mission. As a leader, you exist to carry and promote the fire of the mission for whatever entity you lead. In so doing, you're called to sacrifice on behalf of those you're leading, including the ones who will one day succeed you in carrying the fire. This reality may not be exactly what you had planned as a career option, but I challenge you to remember it: *Sacrifice yields rewards both now and for eternity.*

Fire in the Belly

When a company or ministry is searching for a leader, the leadership usually puts potential candidates through rigorous interviews and personality and aptitude testing, all the while making sure the interviewees have the credentials to fill the position. The company is looking for a leader who has the skills and aptitude to move the entity…dream…vision…mission… forward. Though skills and abilities are critical, I'm not sure they're the most important characteristics of a leader. While a person must have a strong knowledge base and the ability to inspire, train, and motivate people, the most important quality a leader can possess is passion for the mission. Jesus was an incredible example of One who carried the fire of His mission:

> His great purpose sharpened His features, straightened His figure and quickened His step; and sometimes, as He pushed ahead of the Twelve, absorbed in His own thoughts, "they were amazed; and as they followed, they were afraid." Jesus was engaged in a splendid work, whose idea and results touched the imagination of all who were capable of anything noble. He was wholly absorbed in it; and to see unselfish devotion always awakens imitation.[1]

Jesus' commitment and devotion to the mission was so compelling that people couldn't help but be impacted. He carried the fire in His belly, and it warmed whoever came in contact with Him. The disciples were with Jesus for three years. During that time, He taught them everything He could to prepare them for the future. He taught them to pray, fast, lead, heal, and spread the message of the mission. These followers were given the DNA of the mission and, along with it, the message and the power of the Holy Spirit to accomplish all they'd been given to do after Jesus left.

The early church took shape and began to grow because Jesus trained His disciples and they accepted God's call to become His followers. They were serious about the mission, and their passion caught fire and spread to others. Jesus ignited a fire within their hearts that could not be put out. We as Christians in the twenty-first century are evidence that the fire is still burning. The message of the gospel continues to be proclaimed more than 2000 years after the disciples exited planet Earth!

In an article titled "Living in the Vision of God," Christian philosopher Dallas Willard underscores the need to keep the fire within us burning. He tells us how it begins:

> A person of some great inspiration and ability emerges and rises far above his or her origins and surroundings. Perhaps it is a King David of Israel, a Socrates, a St. Anthony or St. Francis, a Martin Luther or a George Fox or a John Wesley. In each of these people there is a...well, a certain "something." They really are different, and that difference explains why these individuals have such great

effect, and why movements and institutions grow up around them. It is as if they stand in another world, and from there they have extraordinary effects in this world—as God acts with them. Organization of their activities takes place, and other organizations spin off from them as numbers of talented individuals are drawn to them and make their lives in their wake. But these other individuals—usually, but not always, very well intending—do not carry the "fire," the "certain something," within them. The mission or missions that have been set afoot begin a subtle divergence from the vision that gripped the founder, and before too long the institution and its mission has become the vision…In most cases, when the original fire dies out, the associated institutions and individuals carry on for a while, increasingly concerned about success and survival, and then they either find another basis to stand upon, or they simply disappear.[2]

We have a limited amount of time to accomplish what we've been given to do. We are not guaranteed "X" number of years on this stage of life and action. One day it will all come to an end. In the meantime, we are God's agents. We've been anointed for the roles we have been given, even if it is for a very short period of time. And we should never forget that we are only here because God has placed us in positions of leadership for a finite period of time. Therefore, in addition to leadership skills, the future leader must carry the "fire for the mission" in his or her belly. That person must feel anointed to carry on the DNA of whatever he or she has been called to lead.

Nothing encourages me more than when I hear younger advisors in our company giving the same advice I would give a client. Or when I hear senior leadership personnel passionately sharing the "Wisdom for Wealth. For Life" message in a more winsome and compelling manner than I do. When I see and hear evidence that they "get it," I know the fire is burning brightly. As a leader focused on the future, make sure you look for the "evidences" that the mission continues in your people.

Leaders who have a fire for the company's goals and vision automatically draw others as followers. Once a vision is cast and caught, it should consume those who are called to keep it alive. If not, the cooling embers of a dying fire will soon be evident. This was part of the challenge I addressed in chapter 2—we must learn the secret to keeping the original fire of a company's mission burning within us or we run the risk of drifting in our message, goals, and passion. You can't pass on something you don't believe and practice yourself.

Passion is one of the greatest characteristics of any leader that must be passed on. Ron Blue passed the compelling mission of Ronald Blue & Co. on to me. It is incumbent on me to make sure the fire for this mission doesn't die out as I pass it on to whomever might lead after me. Those who know me know I "bleed blue." I truly believe in my heart that everyone needs a financial plan in order to experience peace of mind. Hopefully when people see my devotion to this compelling mission, they too will be awakened and want to imitate that mission. The same should be true about the mission or goal of the entity you're leading.

Some time ago I wrote a letter to Ron to express my gratitude for him and the vision he had for the firm. Our company started small. One day Ron mapped it all out on a single napkin at an ice cream shop with his wife. The passion and the fire to see this company begin and help people become freed-up financially was there from the very beginning. Ron's response to my letter was so encouraging because he wrote back, "I pray that the next leader who comes behind you will have the same passion for the firm that you continue to have." He knows the fire is still burning. It's my calling as CEO today to make sure this fire is kindled and kept red-hot for the next generation of leaders who are waiting in the wings, ready and willing to be trained to keep the fire burning.

Stop and think about how the relay takes place with the Olympic torch. It's passed from one runner to another until the fire of that torch is passed around the world. We have a responsibility as God's disciples and servants to keep the fire of His mission, goal, work, and Word alive and burning so others will hear, learn, and continue to do what the disciples did: tell people about the gospel message of Jesus Christ.

The Threat of Drifting

When leaders allow their focus to drift, the passion wanes and the company begins to move in another direction. Arthur Andersen (1885–1947) is a true example of the potential consequences of drifting. His company had a stellar reputation... until it came crashing down in the Enron scandal in the early years of this century. Dallas Willard wrote,

> Arthur Andersen was a man of rock-solid integrity, with a crystal-clear vision of Accounting as

a profession. He built a magnificent accounting firm on strong moral principles. But eventually the people who ran the firm became obsessed with money-making and success, and then with helping clients make money and become successful. Just that, instead of holding those clients responsible ("account-able") to the public good they all professed to serve. These people—who acted in the good name of Arthur Andersen, but without his vision—brought disaster upon themselves and upon thousands of unsuspecting people who depended upon them. Had the moral fire burned in them that burned in Arthur Andersen, that would not have happened. But a false fire of greed and ambition burned in its place. The cuckold of "success" laid its eggs in the nest of service-to-the-public-good, and a monster was hatched that destroyed the nest and all in it.[3]

Jesus never lost sight of His mission. As authors Joel Rosenberg and T.E. Koshy point out in their book *The Invested Life*,

> [Jesus] prayerfully recruited a team of young men. He invested in them. He cared for them like family, loving them with an everlasting, sacrificial love. He led them on spiritual adventures. He modeled a life of intense prayer. He let them see supernatural answers to their prayers. He gave them assignments—to feed the hungry, care for the sick, comfort the brokenhearted, and to preach the good news of the Kingdom of Heaven. He treated them like sons, correcting their mistakes, praising their

successes, and marking their progress. And then he told them to go and invest in others. He told *his* disciples to go make *more* disciples. He told them to build warm and loving and nurturing and spiritually reproducing communities called the local church. And in the process he ignited the greatest spiritual revolution the world has ever seen.[4]

I've told our company leaders that, like Jesus, we need to model these same practices. Our company is about building strong, healthy teams of fully devoted financial advisors whom God can use to impact our clients to change the world. It's about older advisors taking the younger advisors under their wings to care for them, help them grow in their abilities, and help them reproduce their abilities in the lives of other younger advisors.

I've asked our leaders if they can do what Jesus did. Can they love and sacrifice for those they are mentoring? Will they give them assignments that challenge the limits of their ability and be there to correct, teach, encourage, challenge, and praise them along the way? Can they measure their own success by the success of those who are coming after them? This is the only way we can develop the next level of men and women who will one day lead our company. This development pathway requires time, effort, and sacrifice. Without this level of commitment, we are at risk for mission drift.

Sacrifice

The second reason for a leader's existence is summed up in the word *sacrifice*. God calls us to be *living* sacrifices. The apostle Paul wrote, "I urge you...in view of God's mercy, to offer your bodies as a living sacrifice, holy and pleasing to God—this is your true and proper worship" (Romans 12:1).

Sacrifice means "surrender or loss to gain something else; a giving up of a desirable object in behalf of a higher object; to surrender for the sake of something else." What does *surrender* mean? Surrender is "to resign in favor of another; to yield to any influence, passion, or power." Do you catch the thread here? As a leader, we're to surrender and resign to those in authority over us while simultaneously dying to self and giving to those who come after us. *Give* means "to convey to another."

In a recent sermon, Andy Stanley, pastor of NorthPoint Community Church in Atlanta, commented, "The value of a life is always determined by how much of it is given away." I couldn't agree more. As I thought about this, I realized the opposite of *giving* was *keeping*. "To keep" means "to hold; to retain in one's possession; to maintain; not to lose or part with."

Wow! What a contrast. In a nutshell, "I exist to give and not keep all that has been entrusted to me, including knowledge about the mission, how to do financial planning, different responsibilities, decision-making prerogatives, and so on. I exist to work alongside others and not dictate to them what must be done." (This doesn't mean there won't be times when, as the leader, I may need to step in and make a decision.) It means that I lead by allowing others who are part of my team to lead as much as possible. Jesus gave His life so I might live. He was an example of giving and not holding on to power or control. As a leader, that is what I am to do. I am to give of myself to those who come after me so they will be equipped to lead the mission in the future.

Remember, the concept we're centering on right now is that great leaders will be focused on those who will one day take the company mission to the next level. They will not be men and women who are autocratic and dictatorial, people who lord it over those they are leading. To get a grasp on this idea of giving, we need to remember we're not our own. We were bought with a price that Jesus paid (1 Corinthians 6:20). We are owned by God. Just like we give money to acknowledge His ownership, so too we give of ourselves to acknowledge His ownership of us. Giving money breaks the power of money in our lives. Giving of ourselves to those who come after us frees us from this world and our natural tendency to think our lives are all about us.

One of the ways sacrifice works best is when we understand that this planet is not our permanent home. We are sojourners—strangers here for a season and then gone. We have an eternal home. As long as we keep this perspective, we will know how to give and sacrifice and surrender without hesitation.

> By faith Abraham, when called to go to a place he would later receive as his inheritance, obeyed and went, even though he did not know where he was going. By faith he made his home in the promised land like a stranger in a foreign country; he lived in tents, as did Isaac and Jacob, who were heirs with him of the same promise. For he was looking forward to the city with foundations, whose architect and builder is God (Hebrews 11:8-10).

Earth is not our permanent home or our heaven; therefore, we can give up our need to control, our desire to race ahead, and our goal to achieve only what we think is important. There is something much greater at stake here—our call from God to build others up by being disciple makers. We are just passing through this world, and if we want to leave a mark after we're gone, it will be through people in whom we've invested our time, even our very lives.

Leading through sacrifice also prepares us to experience greater freedom. We may have a smaller piece of the pie, but our influence will grow because we're committed to preparing the next generation. In time, they will do the same. After the apostle Paul, Timothy and Titus continued to carry the truth of God to a lost and dying world. And they weren't the only ones! The church today is a testimony of the sacrifices people have made so the mission of Jesus Christ would continue.

4

WHEN YOU GET THE *WHY*

What Why *Looks Like*

Once you understand the *why* of what you do each day, including the need for *sacrifice*, you will quickly move on to incorporate more hallmarks of a great leader.

Learning to Delegate

Far too many leaders want to do everything themselves. And when a leader tries to make every decision and insists on having input in every aspect within a company, he or she is holding back those who could be leading and helping the company grow and become stronger. Delegation, by definition, is "letting someone else do what we've been doing." This is extremely difficult for people who have never come to terms with their egos. As I mentioned in chapter 1, we must deal with our egos or we'll face one disappointment and failure after another.

Until humility is present in the lives of leaders, they will continue to think no one can do the job as well as they can. The leaders will be reluctant to delegate tasks and projects. They will withhold praise and gratitude from employees for fear of being overshadowed. But leaders, especially those in middle management, will not become successful until they are engaged in the *intentional process* of coaching followers to have the ability to work on their own and handle the decision-making responsibilities that have been delegated to them.

Moving responsibilities off our plates and giving them to those who are coming up through the ranks is a freeing experience. This gives us the opportunity to lead and not get caught up in the smaller, more detailed tasks that can fill up our days. We will have the time and energy to continue to set the course of the vision and keep watch over the mission to make sure the company is on target and moving in the right direction.

At Ronald Blue & Co., the key to our business achievements is the success of our financial advisors. When I was a new CEO, I spent the majority of my time mentoring these key individuals. Since they are the most critical group for our business's success, the idea of allowing anyone else to lead them was unnerving to me. I felt I could give away some of the other tasks on my plate, but "surely no one else could lead this group the way I could." However, as my duties expanded, it quickly became obvious I couldn't keep leading this team of individuals the way they needed to be led. After struggling with the decision, I finally decided to delegate the leadership of this group to one of our up-and-coming leaders in the home office. Looking back, I don't know why I waited so long. This man has done a masterful job of leading, and he's taken the group far beyond anything I could have.

Leaders need to let go, to not try to maintain control of everything. Leadership focused on control stifles the next generation and retards their growth. And worst of all, potential successors who have the skill packages to continue to promote the company's vision many times leave because they lose patience waiting for the leader to give them more responsibility.

Great leaders know how to delegate and train those who are coming up behind them. They realize doing all the work will wear them down. Moses' father-in-law, Jethro, challenged him to select men who could help him lead so he wouldn't have such a heavy load to bear (Exodus 18:13-22). But there is more to this than letting people help. Preparing others to lead is the primary way we pass on the company's vision. It's also the way we set the stage for sustainability.

Although there are costs associated with delegating, such as spending time and assets on training, there are multiple rewards for effective delegation. The current leader receives more discretionary time. Future leaders gain a sense of vested interest in the company and increased job satisfaction. The company gains leverage and quicker responsiveness to issues because there isn't the bottleneck of having one person—the primary leader—making all the decisions. I believe that learning to delegate and not being afraid to pass on responsibilities to future leaders has been the most freeing thing I've done in my management roles.

If you delegate and pay the price now, you will get more freedom in the future. You will have more followers helping you keep your mission alive and the fire burning. I'm thrilled with our Executive Leadership Team and the managing directors around the country who run the Ronald Blue & Co. offices. By delegating to them, our firm is stronger, has more impact, and I have more freedom to pursue keeping and promoting our mission.

I must warn you, however, that delegating can't happen without humility and the desire to see other people grow to their maximum potential. The rewards of delegating are substantial! So how do we begin the delegation process?

Do What Only You Can Do

A leader shouldn't do anything someone else can do effectively. This concept will help you stay on track doing what only you can do. To train your company's next leaders, you must be willing to say no to doing jobs or handling responsibilities that can be delegated to someone else on your team. This also allows your followers to step into the spotlight and shine. It enables you to see their skills, talents, and potential as future leaders. You have to let go and teach the people on your team to be effective. You too will develop and grow as you allow others opportunities to lead in various ways.

I've found that one of the ways to implement the concept of letting go is to practice *Management By Absence* (MBA). As you train potential successors and let them do more, an easy way to see that it happens is through your choice to be absent at times. I know leaders who believe they need to be in every meeting or the business won't run correctly. The contrary is true. The business will run better if the leader isn't doing everything—making every decision and attending every meeting.

We recently had some big decisions going on at Ronald Blue & Co. At the same time I unexpectedly needed to make a trip back to Kansas for a family emergency. And guess what—by my being absent, those under me were forced to make decisions and carry on the work of the business without me. And they did a great job! Practicing MBA leadership will help you realize that Charles de Gaulle was correct when he said, "No one is indispensable."

Share the Wealth

I've also found that leaders may need to sacrifice by giving up scheduled increases in income to make sure those following after them are taken care of financially. You may have to sacrifice in this area so that others will benefit from appropriate increases. There are times when I stopped taking raises in my salary so that the managers who reported to me could be better rewarded for their efforts. I didn't do this with the idea of receiving personal gain but rather to make sure I kept my team motivated. I knew if I lost key people it would be difficult to keep the company's mission fire burning. I would run the risk of ending up with a pile of cooling embers instead of a vibrant message. I wanted my leadership team to be red-hot with drive and determination to live out the principles of our mission statement.

There have been many companies that have failed because their leaders were consumed with the idea that making money for themselves and their families was what being in business was about. They continued to make millions while the company went under and those under them lost income and jobs. Remember, it's not about you. It's about disciple making and doing the right things for the betterment of the organization. (Note: To do this, of course, you as the leader need to manage your personal finances in a manner that allows you to be in a position to make this sacrifice.)

The Payoff

There is a cool thing about sacrifice, surrender, giving, and resignation. There *is* something in it for the leaders. When we as leaders give up things like some decision making, income increases, taking on responsibilities, and so forth, we gain more freedom (including time), less risk, inspired followers, and more mission accomplishment. The company has an exponential return. The power of leadership is realized. The leader gives up a desirable object to gain higher results.

As a leader, are you asking, "What can I surrender, resign, or give up to help take the people following me to the next level? What steps can I take to model sacrifice and further our mission?"

Luke records Jesus' words about sacrifice: "Whoever tries to keep their life will lose it, and whoever loses their life will preserve it" (Luke 17:33). This is exactly what Jesus did! He lost His life but received an eternal gain. When we give, we convey our willingness to transfer ownership to God and to those who are being trained by us. But if we seek to cling to, guard, and preserve our positions, we will ultimately lose them.

Earlier I stated that each of us will eventually lose our positions one way or another. Either we will retire, resign, die, or move on for some reason. Training the next generation of leaders ensures that we will make our marks on the future in some way. Here's an unavoidable truth: If we give, we will gain. If we try to keep what really isn't ours, we will lose all. There will be an ending to our story. If we give, we have the opportunity to help write the next chapter as we prepare the next generation to take over.

The apostle Paul instructed Timothy to be strong. Leadership probably didn't come easy for the young man, but he was the one Paul sent into difficult situations. Paul wrote, "The things you have heard me say in the presence of many witnesses entrust to reliable people who will also be qualified to teach others" (2 Timothy 2:2). Paul sent Timothy out as a leader, but he also wanted him to prepare others to be leaders one day. He knew what Jesus knew. In order for the gospel message to continue, men and women had to have a fire, a passion, burning within them to see it continue. This means handing off and passing on the mission so that your organization will continue. Timothy was living in the vision of God. He was doing what we are called to do today:

- To truly lead, you must learn to serve (Matthew 20:25-28; John 12:26).

- To truly gain, you must be willing to lose something (Matthew 10:39; John 12:25).

- To truly receive, you must give (Matthew 10:40-42; Luke 6:38).

- To truly live, you must die (Matthew 16:25; John 12:24).

GREAT LEADERS VS. BAD LEADERS

Which One Will You Become?

My uppermost goal as CEO is to prepare our company and its next generation of leaders for the future and the time when I'll no longer be actively involved. I know the next leader will need to carry the fire of the mission within him or her, just as I do now. I also know he or she will need to have all the requisite skills required of any CEO (the ability to communicate, skill with numbers, wise decision making, and so on). One interesting thing I've noticed is that in any entity, the men and women who emerge as tomorrow's leaders will likely have more skills and abilities than the current leader. And therein lies the greatest distinction between a great leader and a bad leader.

Great Leaders Support the Strengths in Others

Great leaders aren't afraid of the strengths found in others. Bad leaders are intimidated by them. In early 2002, before I'd been named CEO, I sensed that something was about to take place within the leadership ranks of the firm. One night during a Bible study at my house, I looked over at a young guy who was with our firm. I said, "Whatever happens next, don't go anywhere." I knew that if the board named me as the firm's next leader, I wanted this individual to be part of my team.

Why did I want him to be part of my team? During the time he'd been in my Bible study, I'd observed several key attributes. He was much smarter and more educated than me. He was talented with numbers, very articulate, and had solid credentials. Plus he had a strong capacity to lead, which I knew our firm needed if we were going to be an industry leader. I had a choice: I could either bring him in as part of my leadership team and allow him to grow by using his talents and giftedness or I could be intimidated by his strength and look for someone not as skilled and gifted so I would never be challenged. The latter is what bad leaders do. They are intimidated by strength in others so they tend to surround themselves with less talented people. They also look for ways to suppress talented followers, which is counterproductive to building a strong organization.

I could have feared this young man's ability and insight, convincing myself that he would challenge and eventually supersede my leadership. But I refused to let myself fall into that trap. I wanted to leverage his talents and skills for our company. A great leader hires people more gifted and talented than he or she is. Bad leaders invariably stifle talented potential successors, and by so doing retard the growth of the entity they lead. The focus of an effective leader is building up the next generation of leaders, not tearing the company down or inhibiting its potential.

Over the years I've had many opportunities to observe great and bad leadership. I witnessed a church spiral down after initially having a very promising ministry. The senior pastor hired a talented assistant pastor who was eager to serve. Without a doubt the church had a ministry team in place that was effective and energetic. The younger pastor was also an excellent communicator. He began to take on more responsibility in the pulpit. It quickly became obvious that he had the potential to become the next senior pastor if given enough time to grow and mature, but within a short period of time he was gone. Why? Because the senior pastor felt threatened by the younger man's abilities.

Instead of coming alongside him and training him to become his successor, the senior pastor looked for ways to frustrate and discourage the younger pastor. He took over everything and delegated nothing, effectively sabotaging the church's ministry by holding his would-be protégé back. The young pastor left for a place that would allow him to exercise his gifts. Several years passed before this church recovered from the damage done as a result of the senior pastor's insecurity.

Another example of a bad leader was a college coach I knew. This man was intimidated by a player's ability. At first I didn't understand what was taking place. Then I noticed how this man treated that player. He focused on him negatively, belittling him and tearing him down. Bad leaders put down rather than embrace strong, gifted individuals. This coach continued to look for ways to hold the player back rather than empowering him to help the team win.

After reading portions of Walter Isaacson's biography of Steve Jobs, I determined that Jobs had been a polarizing figure, especially when it came to his leadership. Though no one can dispute the fact he founded and led (on two different occasions) a great company that impacted the lifestyle of millions of people, his legacy of leadership isn't so kind. Jobs often intimidated people, called them names, treated them like commodities, took credit for other people's ideas, and made the people around him feel small. While he was brilliant in many ways, he was a poor leader whose extraordinary talents and organizational abilities allowed him the latitude to get away with mistreating others. In his biography of Jobs, Isaacson wrote:

> Jobs speaks candidly, sometimes brutally so, about the people he worked with and competed against. His friends, foes, and colleagues provide an unvarnished view of the passions, perfectionism, obsessions, artistry, devilry, and compulsion for control that shaped his approach to business...Driven by demons, Jobs could drive those around him to fury and despair. But his personality and products were interrelated, just as Apple's hardware and software tended to be, as if part of an integrated system.[1]

The truth is that Apple succeeded *despite* Jobs' flaws.

Unlike Jobs, the college coach, and the senior pastor I referred to earlier, great leaders know that effectively delivering the message and mission of the company centers on their people. Any ministry, business, church, or family is only as successful as the people the leaders train and develop. Joe Gibbs, three-time Super Bowl-winning coach of the Washington Redskins and owner of Joe Gibbs Racing (fielding NASCAR-winning drivers), stated in a letter he wrote to Ronald Blue &

Co.: "I always feel like success in coaching revolves around the right players…Pick the right people and they are going to make you look good…[Therefore, it's wise] to spend your time and your resources picking your people."

In a 2007 edition of *Business-to-Business Magazine*, Mike Pellegrino wrote about the new Alanta Braves general manager, Frank Wren, who was taking over the reins from John Schuerholz: "John's management style is to hire good people and let them do their jobs." In order to build a team for the future, you and I as leaders have to have confidence in the people we hire and give them opportunities to demonstrate their abilities. The best decision we can make is to surround ourselves with capable people—including some who are smarter and quicker than we are. An immature leader will not be eager to do this. And if he or she does, the person hired will be tethered and not allowed to shine brightly for fear he or she will outshine the leader. Frank Wren believes:

> The process clearly starts with good people. It starts with the understanding of the importance of building a team. The importance of empowering your department heads…These people, the ones you surround yourself with, have to know that they are not being second-guessed. They have to know they can make decisions and go forward…You find talent, develop it and put it to the field to compete for a championship every year.[2]

This is what great leaders do. They build winning teams—teams that will endure for generations to come.

A few years back I asked the senior leadership in our home office to be involved in the interview process of every qualified financial planner applicant seeking work with us. This additional layer of interviewing cost Ronald Blue & Co. money and time, but the results have been very positive. It has enabled us to make sure those we hire have the capacity to one day be leaders in the firm.

Great Leaders Have Strong Relational Ability

A great leader is easy to have a relationship with; a bad leader is hard to have a relationship with. Why is this the case? Leaders who are fearful of losing their positions or being overshadowed by others (afraid of the strength in others) will continually be watching their backs. They won't let themselves be vulnerable or get too close. They keep their cards close to the vest and never give up things they know might help someone else, especially potential successors. In doing this, these bad leaders believe they will always be needed. The business relationships they do have will generally be at a surface level only.

God, however, created us for relationships—first with Him and then with people. There are many levels of relationships. Some are very close, while others are friendly but not as personal. Jesus chose twelve disciples, but out of that group only three were His intimate friends—Peter, John, and James. Having too many close associates can be difficult and tiring, but having no close friends will create an atmosphere filled with loneliness and frustration.

When it comes to relationships, inside and outside the office, great leaders need to define the boundaries. We can't train people to become our successors if we never spend time with them in openness and with transparency. These relationships require more relational closeness. We must spend time with our people training, coaching, mentoring, and doing whatever preparing for leadership looks like in our entities. This isn't to imply that we need to do everything with our followers. I do very little, if anything, outside the work environment with those I lead. However, when I'm with them at work, I'm "all in" and engaged with them. I'm also close enough to them to know how they're doing in regard to their families and other relationships. I'm concerned for them and care for them—and not just as employees. This perspective helps me be a holistic mentor to our next-generation leaders.

Great Leaders Provide Clear Communication

Great leaders provide clear and concise communication. Bad leaders have poor communication patterns, making them confusing and hard to understand. They make it difficult for their followers to know exactly what's going on. They seem to hold important information back or don't come clean with all the issues. They tend to be less up front. They like to triangulate with others on the team. You're never sure if what you see is what you actually get.

Joe Gibbs, former Washington Redskins coach and current owner of JGR Racing, had more to say on leadership in his letter to Ronald Blue & Co.: "One of the key aspects of being a coach [leader] is realizing we must be great communicators; it is the responsibility of the coach [leader] to be sure that all players on the team understand the objectives and the plan on how to achieve them." A great leader leads by making sure that those who work with him or her understand why they're doing what they're doing. Great leaders are straightforward and direct in their communication style.

A good illustration of clear vs. vague communication could occur at Ronald Blue & Co. around vacation time in December. Because of the heightened planning that goes on at the end of the year for our clients, December is very busy for us. If I don't want my followers to take vacations during the month of December, I need to clearly state that instead of saying something like, "I'd rather you not take vacation." The more casual statement leaves the door open for interpretation because it's vague, which might result in frustration if the follower takes a vacation when he or she is really needed at work.

A Great Leader Accepts Feedback

Because great leaders don't fear strength in others, they can listen and accept feedback without feeling threatened. Great leaders value offered input even when it's not what they want to hear or they disagree with the opinion. Bad leaders, on the other hand, tend to be threatened and go on the defensive, ignoring advice that's contrary to what they think. These types of leaders tend to surround themselves with "yes" men and women. Bad leaders listen to only what makes them feel good. They misinterpret loyalty as agreement.

Since few employees buck or question or disagree with bad leaders, the leaders consider their people loyal followers. If a follower disagrees, he or she is labeled "disloyal." A vicious cycle then ensues. No one tells the truth; everyone is afraid to disagree with the leader; employees appear to be loyal. It's been my experience that the contrary is true. It's usually those employees who are willing to disagree with their leaders that are the most loyal to the mission. That's why they're willing to go out on a limb by speaking up. Their loyalty to the mission compels them to confront and give input when they sense something could be improved.

Great leadership is characterized by two things. First, a willingness to allow others to identify the leader's opportunities to grow and, second, a commitment by the leader to help followers develop their unrealized potential. Great leaders do not fear criticism by others or the strengths and insights people offer.

There is a great story in the Bible that gets to the heart of accepting input. The king of Israel and the king of Judah (Jehoshaphat) were aligned to go into battle together. King Jehoshaphat asked the king of Israel to inquire of the Lord as to whether or not they would have success if they did so. Would they win the war? So the king of Israel asked 400 prophets if they should go to battle or not. The prophets agreed that Israel and Judea should definitely go into battle, and that Israel would win.

Jehoshaphat, however, was still concerned. "Is there no longer a prophet of the Lord here whom we can inquire of?"

The king of Israel said there was this other guy named Micaiah, but he hated him "because he never prophesies anything good about me, but always bad" (1 Kings 22). Basically, the king of Israel was saying, "I don't want to hear from this prophet because he doesn't tell me what I want to hear."

Jehoshaphat was appalled, so the king of Israel summoned Micaiah. When he arrived, he was told what the other prophets had told the king. The messenger said, "Let your word agree with theirs, and speak favorably" (verse 13).

There was tremendous pressure on the prophet to stick with the party line and be a yes-man. So what did Micaiah do? At first he tells the king what he wants to hear—that he will be successful in battle. But the king of Israel does something that every great leader should do. He says to Micaiah, "How many times must I make you swear to tell me nothing but the truth in the name of the Lord?" In other words, "Micaiah, what do you really think? Give it to me straight."

So that is what the prophet does. He gives it to him straight, countering what the other 400 prophets had said. Micaiah tells the king they will be defeated if they go into battle. He tells the truth.

Predictably, the king of Israel does what bad leaders do. He ignores the advice. The king orders Micaiah to be put in prison and fed sparingly until the king returns from battle. But the king never returns because Micaiah's advice was right. The king of Israel died from wounds sustained in battle.

This is an example of why listening to contrary advice can be so critical to the success of any leader. Having people around you who will tell you the truth is a form of protection and a tremendous sign of excellent leadership and terrific "followership." No leader should want "yes" employees!

Followers who are loyal to the vision and care passionately about a company, firm, or organization will not be afraid to give advice even though they know the leader might not like it.

Great leaders create environments where input—even contrary input—is welcomed and listened to. Bad leaders won't even have those "negative" folks around them. And when they do come, they usually don't stay in the organization long. They are either replaced or silenced in some manner.

The Essence of Great Leaders

Outstanding leaders willingly lay themselves aside and concentrate on the mission rather than on their personal goals. The leadership style of Jesus was based on helping others grow and perform to the best of their abilities. That should be our *modus operandi* as well—promoting the success of others rather than promoting ourselves. We need to value others above ourselves (Philippians 2:3). God is the great promoter. He raises people to their positions (Luke 14:7-11). We shouldn't seek great things for ourselves, including promotions, accolades, being singled out for praise. We need to focus on the mission God gives us and the people He puts in our paths...

and let *God* single us out if He chooses. "Let someone else praise you, and not your own mouth; an outsider, and not your own lips" (Proverbs 27:2).

We have a choice of where we direct our focus: on others or ourselves. Great leaders focus on others.

6

A ROAD TRIP THROUGH POTHOLES

How Great Leaders Lead

M y wife, Julie, and I were excited to get the car packed and hit the road. We'd been planning this trip for months. It had two purposes. First, we would be able to visit some of the Ronald Blue & Co. offices around the country. This would give us a chance to thank the team for a job well done since I'd been appointed CEO and allow us to meet many of the team members for the first time. Second, we'd just sent our youngest off to college, so this trip would be a distraction from thinking about our "empty nest." Julie had told me this was going to be a hard time for her, so this seemed like a good way to get her mind off the end of that season of our lives.

We packed our convertible to the gills for the six-week trip and left the first week of September 2008. That time frame may jog something in your memory. It was a tumultuous year in finance. One week into our trip, the U.S. markets began to unravel. Lehmann Brothers, a prominent securities firm, filed for bankruptcy, and it only got worse from there. Every day seemed to bring a new crisis. What followed over the next few months would later become known as "The Great Recession."

Almost six months later, on March 9, 2009, the financial markets dropped roughly 40 percent in value.

Needless to say our trip wasn't as relaxing as we'd hoped. I spent many hours on conference calls back to the home office as we calmed clients and staff during the unexpected- and unprecedented-in-our-time market upheaval. This situation allowed me to model one of the key characteristics that should be modeled by every leader. In this chapter we'll discuss this characteristic and look at several other qualities that should be evident in how a great leader leads.

Isopraxism

Right now you're probably wondering what *isopraxism* is. I'd never heard or even seen the word until I was reading a *Sports Illustrated* article that explained it. *Isopraxism* is an anthropological explanation of how athletes pull toward the same energy in team sports. In our terms, if one person, especially the leader, gets discouraged or feels defeated, the entire group will be affected. For example, if the quarterback in a football game gets rattled and shows his disappointment by hanging his head because a receiver dropped a pass, the rest of the team will take their cue from him and become discouraged as well. If a baseball player makes an error, the pitcher's response usually reveals how the team will react to the misplay.

Wow! I thought. This is exactly the same principle we find in the business world. People in leadership roles have multiple opportunities to respond either negatively or positively to the potholes that inevitably occur in any business, ministry, family, or other enterprise. Though I was unfamiliar with the term *isopraxism* at the time, the market collapse of 2008–09 gave me a golden opportunity to practice it. Our staff members were looking to me to see how I would respond so they could know the direction we were going to take. Was I going to be worried, negative, stressed, depressed, or anxious? Or was I going to be positive, maintain a solid perspective, take it one day at a time, and be upbeat?

The Ronald Blue & Co. team was watching me, and just like team players respond to their pitcher or quarterback, my team would respond to me in like manner. If I kept my head up, shoulders back, and showed a rock-solid confidence and hope in God, they would more than likely do the same. If I slumped, had a sour face, and exhibited anxiety, they would follow suit.

During the drives between Atlanta, Seattle, Los Angeles, Houston, and then back home to Atlanta, I encouraged, exhorted, and challenged our team members to maintain their upbeat perspective. I reminded them of previous financial slumps we'd come through and asked them to recall other potholes we'd weathered in the 28-year history of the firm. Those included the market crash of 1987 and failed expansion strategies in 1994 and 2000. The abilities to maintain composure in the midst of serious challenges, remain consistent, and provide positive leadership and perspective are key traits of any strong leader.

Part of *isopraxism* includes encouraging team members to keep going. To "recover at the speed of the game" or, in my case, "the speed of the business." As leader I needed to model the fortitude, courage, and faith of continuing on with the mission. For example, one of our partners works with several professional athletes who are the genesis of this concept. When they get knocked down in football, they get back up. If they give up a home run, they don't dwell on it. Instead, they move to the next pitch. In business, this simply means that when the inevitable potholes occur and jolt the company, the leader continues on and encourages his or her followers to get up and move forward. When we're knocked off center, we get up quickly and take the next step to keep the company, ourselves, and our team members moving.

One of the main reasons leaders can practice *isopraxism* in the midst of difficulty is because the passion of the mission burns so deeply within them that they can't help but press on. Jesus did this very thing. He kept His focus on His Father and the mission set before Him. Yes, He expressed His emotions, but His emotions were always set in the context of who He was and what He was called to do. You may think, "Well, He had the advantage of being the Son of God," which is true. But the truth is, if we have accepted Him as our Savior, the Holy Spirit is alive within us. We can go through times of discouragement and not really flinch because we know God is at work bringing all things together for the good of those who love Him (Romans 8:28).

The financial situation of this country continues to be rocky with constant ups and downs. As the leader of Ronald Blue & Co., one aspect of my job in this time of volatility is to make sure we don't lose sight of our original mission. Many times leaders take their eyes off their missions to look at the storms around them, and this can lead to negative outcomes for the enterprises they're leading. Peter experienced this when he walked on the water with Jesus. He was okay even though the storm was raging as long as he focused on Jesus. When he took his focus off Jesus, he sank.

By being aware of *isopraxism*, I set the stage and the atmosphere for my leadership team and other team members to fulfill our mission. As I mentioned, people who know me know I bleed blue. I believe everyone needs a financial plan in order to experience financial peace of mind. Hopefully, when my team members see my devotion to this compelling mission, they will want to imitate it. Catching this vision and passing it on keeps our company strong from the inside out. When difficulties hit or we have to deal with the harsh reality of our country's finances, we can do it as a team because we're all compelled by our mission to help people apply God's wisdom to their financial situations.

How You Lead Is Important

Although *who* you are as a leader is as important as *why* you're leading (the mission), *how* you lead may be the most important aspect of all. *How* you lead reveals the core motivation of your heart. When Nehemiah went to Jerusalem to spearhead rebuilding the city wall, we're told how men were committed to the rebuilding project. Then amid the list of workers and repairs we see something we haven't seen yet—a description of *how* one particular builder worked. Nehemiah wrote, "Next to him, Baruch son of Zabbai *zealously* repaired another section" (Nehemiah 3:20). Obviously this particular person was doing his job well, and his work stood out so much the writer included that comment. There were at least twenty-five other builders mentioned before Baruch, and at

least twelve others are listed after Baruch. But Baruch was the
only one highlighted for *how* he was doing what he was doing.

So let's look at some key characteristics for the *how* of great
leadership.

Passionate

Baruch was *passionate* about his bricklaying. He laid bricks
day in and day out. He threw himself into what must have
seemed like a mundane task to others. Isn't this the case with
most jobs—even for those in leadership positions? Many work-
days consist of doing the same activity over and over again. It's
how we handle this monotony that speaks volumes to those
we're leading. Do we continue to be passionate about our tasks
even if it seems like the "same old stuff"? Are we zealous about
the basics of our business or do we only get passionate when
we're involved in a new project, challenge, process, client, or
strategic endeavor? Can we spend days doing mundane work
in a passionate manner because it too leads to fulfilling the mission? If not, this could be a problem because, whether we're
aware of it or not, our teams are watching us.

As CEO, I must often deal with the same issues over and
over, such as planning problems, people conflicts, and a myriad
of meetings. Many times I feel like the Bill Murray character in
the movie *Groundhog Day*. He's forced to live the same day over
and over again. However, if I want to be singled out by God as
Baruch was, I need to throw myself into the tasks at hand—not
just the exciting times of strategic planning and growth, but the
mundane, day-to-day ones too.

To remain passionate and zealous, I do a couple things. First,

I maintain a few client relationships so I never forget what our company does to assist people. Second, Julie and I meet frequently with couples to assist them with their finances. Sometimes this involves budgeting, other times it's about investments, and at times it centers on cash-flow planning. Regardless of what we're dealing with, when I see marriages and families impacted positively by getting their financial houses in order, I can't help but be passionate and zealous about the mission of helping people attain financial peace of mind.

This passionate principle is true with my family as well. Am I as excited in the day-to-day workings of my children's lives, which may include school, homework, laundry, dinner, and carpooling, as I am about an upcoming family vacation? Are Mondays and Thursdays as exciting as Saturdays? They should be. We may be tempted to see some things—like a son's or daughter's soccer game as being routine and mundane, but it's not to him or her. That's why consistent, constant, and passionate leadership is so important. Those we're leading are watching us. And as leaders, our passion is contagious. If handled correctly, it will influence the next generation and ensure our mission remains alive and vibrant.

Tenacious

In addition to being passionate, Baruch was *tenacious*. He didn't throw in the towel no matter how boring, tough, or demanding the job was. *Tenacious* is a good word. It denotes strength, courage, and determination. The mental picture that comes to my mind is that of a dog with a coveted stick in his mouth and I'm trying to pry it out of his mouth. Do you have the picture? The harder I pull and shake the stick, the more the dog sinks in his teeth, determined to not let go. As leaders, we need to model this characteristic to our followers. *Tenacious* is an attitude that never quits.

"Pain is temporary, but quitting is forever." Have you heard that saying before? First Corinthians 15:58 is a great verse that confirms this truth. "Be steadfast, immovable, always excelling in the work of the Lord, because you know that in the Lord your labor is not in vain (NASB)." When the mission remains the main focus, the efforts of the leader will not be in vain.

The principle of tenacious leadership plays out in the family realm too. Many times Mom and Dad may feel like throwing in the towel. They wonder if their time and effort spent training their children are worth it. At times, their efforts seem fruitless. Perhaps you're wondering that right now about your family. Your children aren't making good decisions, and they just don't seem to understand what you're trying to teach them. Julie and I have been in that very spot. Many times we wondered if we were good parents. At times we felt like giving up and not "fighting for our kids." But looking back now, our decision to be tenacious was one of the best ones we've made. We are so thankful we stayed the course and fought for our boys against Satan and the pull of the world. Over the past couple of years, each of our boys has thanked us for fighting for them.

This same principle of tenaciousness applies to any enterprise you lead as well as to your family. Tenacity is needed, and your efforts will not be in vain. Pass this trait on to those you lead, and you'll see abundant results from this wise attitude.

Enthusiastic

Baruch was also *enthusiastic*, which is essential to strong leadership. In fact, when people see our energetic mindsets and our passions, they will be more likely to catch our vision and mission. And there's no doubt about it: Just like passion, enthusiasm is contagious!

Whereas passion is rooted deep in the psyche of an individual, enthusiasm is how it's manifested externally. One of my sons works for a company that does elementary school fund-raising. Their entire model works because of the enthusiasm their team brings into the classrooms. The kids love the presentation, and so do the teachers and parents. Why? Because it's upbeat, contains a "can-do" message, and is presented with an energetic mind-set that rubs off on the kids. They get excited about raising money and winning prizes for each lap they run on "fun run" day. I've observed one of those days, and I must say that the enthusiasm demonstrated by the team leaders moves the entire crowd.

As a leader you can simply go through the motions or you can lead with zeal and enthusiasm. In the book of Acts, we read that Phillip "ran" up to a chariot to share the gospel with an Ethiopian eunuch (8:30). Are you "running" in your position of leadership or just putting in the time by going through the motions? Great leaders need to understand that *how* they lead is every bit as important as *why* they're leading.

More Characteristics of Great Leaders

I've found the following characteristics usually reside within the hearts and souls of great leaders. They need to be passed on to the next generation!

Single-Mindedness (Philippians 3:13)

The ability to stay focused on the one thing that's most important to accomplishing the mission is vital. At Ronald Blue & Co. we must never forget that the main job we do is provide comprehensive planning to help people gain peace of mind. When I became CEO, I made sure we were focused on this goal. Our theme was "Back to the Future."

As your organization's leader, it's incumbent on you to never forget the main mission and keep it the primary goal. If you're the leader of your family, the same is true there. At the end of the day, you're raising young men and women you want to become good, effective members of society and, if God wills, loving husbands and wives. This is why we as parents do the hard work of "discipling" our children when they're young, even though it seems tiring and endless at times.

Avoids Entanglements (2 Timothy 2:4)

Avoiding entanglements is a *learned* skill. This is the ability to not become too busy, which requires simplifying our lives and decluttering them by saying no to some things so we can stay focused on the main mission. People at my office like to joke that I have the gift of "intentional neglect." I have the ability to say no and neglect many *good* things so I can stay focused on the *best* thing—our mission.

Follows God's Principles (2 Timothy 2:5)

All great leaders must have the utmost integrity. They must be trustworthy even in small things, such as expense reports and paying taxes (business and personal).

Works Hard (2 Timothy 2:6)

Great leaders model a strong work ethic. They're diligent and not slothful. Early in my career I made business trips to the West Coast to see several clients. Many days were 16 to 18 hours long, and the powerful work ethic I'd learned as a boy on the farm served me well. Today as CEO, the staff observes me working hard as I see clients, speak on behalf of the firm, meet with next-generation leaders, and fulfill my work-related obligations.

Now, this doesn't mean I'm advocating burning the candle at both ends. I'm not promoting 60- to 80-hour workweeks as the norm. Psalm 127:2 says, "In vain you rise early and stay up late, toiling for food to eat—for [the LORD] grants sleep to those he loves." As discussed earlier, being absent from the enterprise at times can be useful in the training of management personnel. That said, next-generation leaders need to see us working hard and not being lazy. And that goes for home too. Our children need to see us working diligently at home so they will develop a good work ethic and understand responsibility.

Travels Light (Acts 28:30)

Great leaders don't get bogged down by carrying a lot of commitments outside their family and the enterprise they're leading. I have several outside commitments: church, neighborhood activities, boards of directors meetings, and so on, but I'm careful to not get overburdened. I say no to a lot of activities and responsibilities, and I am always careful not to overextend myself. This requires constant monitoring (and getting input from my wife). Over the years I've learned that if I take on a new commitment, I have to decide what goes off the list. Traveling light is essential if we want to have the necessary time to be effective leaders and mentors.

Continues to the End (2 Timothy 3:14)

Great leaders don't lose heart. They continue on course until the baton is passed. Even though they get tired and face obstacles, they don't quit until a successful transition is made to the next generation of leaders. We recently saw this modeled in one of our branch offices. Once the successor had been chosen, there was an 18-month overlap and training period until the handoff was completed. This allowed for continuity, constant mentoring, and input when needed as the new leader took the reins.

Consistent and Constant (Acts 17:17)

Excellent leaders never waver in their message. They are consistently and constantly proclaiming the vision of the entity they're leading. Patrick Lencioni, in his book *The Four Obsessions of an Extraordinary Executive*, wrote: "In order to communicate something adequately, it has to be communicated so many times that the people doing the communicating think they are beating a dead horse."[1] When I read this, I was very encouraged. Often it seems like all I do is communicate the history, purpose, values, and mission of Ronald Blue & Co. to the next generation. I repeat it again and again in many venues, including company meetings, semiannual firm communications, and CEO Roundtable and Conclave events for new hires.

The discipline of "over communicating organizational clarity," as Lencioni calls it, is a key characteristic of any great leader because it helps keep the fire burning for the mission. So even though we may feel like a stuck record at times, that's part of our job as leaders. Effective communication is consistent and repetitive.

Life Is Cyclical

As I write this book, to date we've not had another crisis as difficult as the economic upheaval during that road trip Julie and I took in 2008. However, I know that life is cyclical, especially in business, ministry, and family. Good times are inevitably followed by tough times. Life isn't linear; therefore, I expect to have more opportunities to further strengthen the characteristics I've listed in this chapter. How I lead through the potholes of life will continue to be tested and observed by my team members and those coming behind me. It's critical for the next generation of leaders to see me leading in a way that makes sure our mission is carried on. I need to show them how to lead so when it's their turn, they will be ready.

How about you? Have you considered *how* you lead?

THE FUTURE LEADER

7

CHARACTERISTICS OF A SUCCESSOR

What to Look for in NextGen Leaders

N ow that we've examined the traits necessary to excel as leaders, I'd like to shift gears and consider the characteristics to look for as we seek individuals who will carry the fire for our organizations' missions into the future. When evaluating leadership potential, it's easy to focus on the highly visible attributes and skills, such as analytical brilliance, charisma, ability to present information well, and the drive to succeed. However, these aren't necessarily sure signs of leadership ability. Instead, we need to look for *actions, decisions,* and *behaviors* that reveal true leadership potential consistent with the concepts we've discussed.

There are ten key characteristics to look for as we seek to hire and mentor individuals to serve with us and eventually become leaders in our organizations.

Fire in the Belly

Just as having "fire in the belly" is important for us in our roles as leaders, it's equally important that those who will lead in the future are capable of this same passion. What does "fire in the belly" look like? It's evidenced by eyes that light up when talking about what he or she gets to do every day. It's a willingness to pitch in to help advance the mission wherever and whenever a need exists. It's serving on committees, investing time in newer employees to help them get up to speed, and volunteering to speak on the company's behalf. It's seeing his or her clients recommend your business to their friends because they feel well-served and are caught up in the enthusiasm and passion of the individual serving them. It's building a pipeline of potential employees because folks are drawn to the person's passion for what he or she does so they want in. If your employee exhibits an incessant drive to shape the external environment and make progress in a way that advances the mission of your organization, that's a sure sign there's "fire in that belly."

When I first started at Ronald Blue & Co., I was willing to go anywhere at any time to share about the company. I spoke to groups as small as two (at a seminar where only one couple showed up. I sat down with them, and we had an informal time of sharing). I've also spoken to groups as large as 40,000. To this day, because of the fire that burns within me, I feel compelled to share our mission in differing venues, from college finance classes to career days for seniors, from Sunday school classes to groups of donors for various ministries. I look for this "go anywhere anytime to anyone" mindset in future leaders.

"Big Picture" Thinking

"Big picture" thinkers have the ability and the intellectual capacity to see ambiguous, complex, nonquantifiable situations from a broader view or in a broader context than the one in which they work on a daily basis. They're able to recognize the ramifications of actions taken or decisions made within their immediate work environment, *and* within the broader organization, *and* in the external business environment. For example, in the financial advisory business, "big picture" thinking is evidenced when an advisor understands how a potential new hire on their team could negatively impact another area, such as marketing. The advisor realizes there are limited resources and understands his or her new hire may preclude the Marketing Department hiring someone in their area.

Signs of "big picture" thinkers include demonstrating a curiosity about subjects outside their areas of expertise. They desire to work with an interdisciplinary team in order to bring their thinking to bear on initiatives that impact the entire company. These are individuals who see gaps—whether in systems, tools, resources, or whatever—and come to meetings with possible solutions. They look at industry and cultural changes and then propose suggestions to "get ahead or stay ahead of the curve" so the organization will be in a good position for what's coming down the road.

Early in my career I was continually making notes on ways our company could be improved. One day I took my list of "big picture" thinking to Ron. Much to my surprise, he said, "Why don't you implement those ideas as the new chief operations officer (COO)? I want to promote you to that position." Needless to say, I was surprised! But now as CEO, I better appreciate where Ron was in his thinking and why he promoted me at that time. As the current leader of the firm, I appreciate those who come up with ideas to help the company. And it's a great way for a next-generation person to get on my short list of potential leaders.

Quick and Continual Learning

Let's face it. The world is changing, and so is the business environment in which we operate. If we're going to build our organizations in a manner that will position them well for the future, we need to be raising up next-generation leaders who are on passionate quests to learn and grow. These people are able to absorb knowledge quickly, determine how it applies to the business, and effectively communicate what they've learned to others in a manner that's relevant and on point. They are constantly recommending good books or forwarding articles of interest to the people around them, including the leaders. These lifelong learners are intellectually honest enough to recognize and acknowledge when they don't have the answers, and they are intellectually *curious* enough to go out and find them.

To this day I read books that enable me to be a better leader in our financial services business. I do one or two book reports per year that I forward to my leadership team, along with ideas and concepts that might improve the business or encourage them that our company is on the right track. The saying that "leaders are readers" is true!

Emotional Intelligence

Emotional intelligence quotient (EQ) is a person's ability to identify, assess, understand, and effectively work through his or her own emotions, as well as the emotions of others. Without a certain level of EQ, it's extremely difficult to bring influence to bear within an organization. If a person is unable to influence others, his or her ability to lead will be severely compromised. (In the next chapter we'll discuss this in more detail.)

People who have strong EQ have the ability to get along with, work with, and motivate people to get jobs done. They understand people's buying habits (what will move them to action), and they can present information in a manner that takes into consideration the way others think, how they like to receive information, and what other factors may be important to help them understand, get comfortable with, and buy into what is being considered. Strong EQ is what allows individuals to effectively navigate organizational politics which, whether we like to admit it or not, all companies have. While having a level of self-awareness is an important aspect of being emotionally intelligent, EQ in a business sense is primarily an "others focused" way of thinking and interacting.

So what does emotional intelligence look like in business? People with strong EQ bring new ideas to the table and gain buy-in from impacted parties despite the varied interests and backgrounds of the group as a whole. They tend to have followers because they've already convinced some people to buy into their ideas or initiatives. When they have new ideas that may be tough to sell, they're willing to spend the extra time to provide more information and more support to help people get comfortable with the new direction. The people involved feel the person in charge listens to them, values them, and understands them.

Early in my career I didn't have strong emotional intelligence. I felt my intellect and thinking skills were enough, and when necessary I could force my ideas into practice. I thought office politics was a waste of time, so I didn't expend much effort getting folks to buy into my ideas. In retrospect, EQ was a characteristic I needed to develop to prepare me to become a strong leader. I believe that's one of the primary reasons I had that ten-year wilderness experience before becoming CEO. Today I'm much more in tune with the emotional dynamics going on within the company. As a result, I'm more effective in mobilizing our teams to accomplish our mission and goals. Overall intelligence is certainly important, but when choosing the next generation of leaders EQ is even more critical to success.

Solid Thinking Skills

We've already discussed the concepts of being passionate about learning and capable of "big picture" thinking, so are you wondering, "Aren't those part of 'solid thinking' skills?" "Solid thinking skills" incorporates the ideas of taking what is seen in the "big picture" *and* what has been learned intellectually, and applying this knowledge to form practical, workable plans that are actionable within the business.

Solid thinkers are proficient at thinking analytically *and* thinking creatively and intuitively, which gives them the ability to understand how things actually work within the organization and the pace at which change can be managed and new ideas implemented. In other words, solid thinking takes the ethereal and nebulous and makes it concrete and doable. A leader's solid thinking enables the organization to make decisions and move forward without overanalyzing change or experiencing paralysis.

An illustration of this occurred at our company shortly after the market downturn of October 2008. We knew going into 2009 that revenue would be down due to the markets, so the leadership team made the decision to cancel the annual advisor meeting. We didn't dwell on it by overanalyzing. We knew the money saved by not having this event could be used to invest in our people during the downturn, plus it would allow the advisors to remain in their offices to serve clients, who were very nervous. Solid thinking was evidenced by not overthinking the idea of canceling the meeting, factoring in a myriad of details, and then making a clear and quick decision. If I remember correctly, the process took only a couple of hours to decide.

Another tangible sign of solid thinking skills in potential leaders is their ability to anticipate where you, as leader, are taking the company and getting there one step ahead of you. Next-generation individuals see what's happening directionally, think ahead, and then provide any information required—often before you realize you need it. At Ronald Blue & Co., our management team calls this "Anticipatory Followership." I can tell you from experience that it's a wonderful thing to have folks on your team who have this ability.

Strong Character and Integrity

These traits go almost without saying because they are a must for any great leader—present and future. If there is any question regarding the character or integrity of a next-generation leader candidate, that is a red flag against letting him or her advance in the organization.

At Ronald Blue & Co., we're constantly observing our

potential next-generation leaders to make sure their walks match their talk. Are they consistent and constant in what they do? When difficulties come or they're temporarily knocked off center, do they remain rock-solid in their actions and responses? This is one reason we require our advisors to have their personal financial plans done each year by another advisor, who then submits documentation to our Human Resources Department verifying they're in good standing financially. This is one way we ensure that our advisors practice what we preach.

Drive

We're going to spend a bit more time discussing this character trait because it can manifest itself in two significantly different ways, which I refer to as "Drive Redeemed" (positive) and "Drive Fallen" (negative). Although the behaviors and manifestations can be similar, the motivations vary greatly.

Drive Fallen. "So when you give to the needy *[or do or accomplish X, Y, or Z in the business world],* do not announce it with trumpets, as the hypocrites do...to be honored by others. Truly I tell you, they have received their reward in full" (Matthew 6:2). This is an example of "Drive Fallen." The hypocrites were driven to do specific things and perform certain works so that others would notice and praise them for it. This is *not* the kind of drive we're looking for in future leaders.

Drive Redeemed. This drive is reflected in one of my favorite passages in Scripture: "Whatever you do, *work heartily, as for the Lord and not for men*, knowing that from the Lord you will receive the inheritance as your reward. You are serving the Lord Christ" (Colossians 3:23-24 ESV). We are called to do our very best in all circumstances. This passage implies working hard, training, striving for excellence, focusing, giving our best effort, and recognizing that much is at stake. Our striving isn't for earthly rewards but for *heavenly* ones. Our motivation is to please our Lord. This is the type of drive we need to look for in future leaders. "Drive Redeemed" people don't care who gets the credit.

I had tremendous drive when I started in the financial services business. However, my drive was very much "I" focused. I wanted to get any credit I felt I deserved, and I didn't care who I ran over in the process. I tooted my own horn to make sure folks knew who was behind the idea or action being implemented. My motivation was to lift up myself vs. lifting up the company.

Time, however, has been a great teacher. Today I still have a strong drive, but now I focus on giving credit to others instead of highlighting my part. When people ask me what I do for a living, I simply say, "I work at Ronald Blue & Co." I don't lead with my title and position. By God's grace my drive has been redeemed, and I know those with whom I work are very grateful for the change.

Drive in the Workplace

Let's consider further what *drive* looks like in the workplace. Men and women who are driven from within to succeed thrive in environments where they're able to come together with diverse groups of high-caliber people to tackle complex problems or issues. They invariably redefine their own job descriptions, often forcing their leaders to refine their job descriptions too. People with "Drive Redeemed" are constantly thinking ahead, planning for the future. They often have a clear methodology to continue to build new skills and hone personality traits to achieve their dreams of what they want to become.

Be forewarned! At some point these folks may outshine you until they eventually reach their potential within the organization. As we discussed in an earlier chapter, you shouldn't view this as a threat or be afraid of strength in others. This is *not* a bad thing if you're leading with an eye toward succession. It's simply something to be aware of—and try to embrace—when you have a high-potential, hardworking individual in your midst.

You will also see a solid work ethic in individuals with drive. They keep going until the job is done. They have the ability to deliver on time and in an extraordinary fashion. When thrown a curveball, they view the obstacle as an opportunity to problem-solve or master new skills. They recognize that sometimes they'll fail, but they don't let themselves get stuck there. They pick themselves up, try to learn the lessons they need to from the failure, and get moving again. They are strong, determined, tenacious, and courageous.

Because men and women with drive are so good at delivering results, it can be tempting to overlook the character flaws referenced in "Drive Fallen," so I encourage you, as you consider men and women for leadership roles within your business, to look beyond the results—which are usually stellar—and gain insights into their heart motivation. Having individuals in leadership roles who have the wrong motivation can do great harm to the business. You're looking for drive that doesn't care who gets the credit. Drive covered in humility.

Others Focused

People who are "others focused" have an innate desire to help people succeed. Though they're very capable in their own right, they see sharing what they've learned as an investment in those coming up behind them. They enjoy working on teams and, as just discussed, aren't worried about who gets the credit as long as the goal is reached.

To evaluate this characteristic, you need to look at the person's ambition. Is it clearly for a leadership role, which *requires* focus on others? Or is it oriented toward making individual contributions? Does the individual take pride in accomplishing goals on the basis of his or her own abilities or talk about bringing together and motivating others to achieve those goals together? Is there evidence that he or she is able to create a desire in others to follow him or her? Or are their team members discontent or leaving the company? Does he or she have confidence in the people on the team, providing team members with opportunities to demonstrate their abilities?

At Ronald Blue & Co. we routinely conduct "360-degree reviews" to gain insights into how our folks are actually doing in this area. What do those who are above, below, and beside them in the organization really think about their leadership? We then use these results to develop and train them to be better leaders in their department or division. As a matter of fact, I even have our Human Resources department do a 360 on me every couple of years. This anonymous review allows me to receive candid feedback from those I'm leading, as well as from the management committee, to determine areas in which

I can improve. One way to determine if a person is really others focused is to ask the others.

Business Savvy

Unlike "big picture" and solid thinking that we discussed earlier, "business savvy" is the ability to understand the business in its entirety with a keen eye toward staying in business. Individuals with business savvy comprehend the total picture of the business—how it makes money and how the various parts (divisions, departments, and the like) need to come together to accomplish the organization's mission and financial objectives.

People with business savvy realize the need to balance the competing demands of growth, risk management, capital allocation, expense expansion, and so forth. They also show the aptitude to make decisions in these areas to keep the business healthy. These folks understand the critical ingredients to maintaining the health of the entity, and they never lose sight of them. In our business, one measurement we use is the number of financial advisors we have on our team. Is that number growing? Are we retaining them? Are we losing them? Your business has success metrics for health as well. Your next-generation leaders need to exhibit an understanding of these factors as well as a solid grasp on how to positively impact them for the good of the company.

Bias Toward Action

One of the things I like to say is, "Strategic thinking is good; strategic planning is better; but strategic *action* is best!" Ronald

Blue & Co. is a planning firm, so it could be easy to get caught up in the process of planning and trying to make sure everything is perfect. But because we have a *bias toward action*, we avoid that pitfall. This isn't to say we don't go through a planning process. We do, but we consciously resist the temptation to overplan. Once a plan is set, we get to work. A *bias toward action* is evident when a leader knows when to stop planning and when to start implementing.

When evaluating this characteristic in individuals you believe have leadership potential, observing their ability to build a plan and then implement that plan is crucial. Many times individuals will overanalyze and never get to the implementation. Since the area of decision making is always bigger than the area of knowledge, analysis paralysis can set in. The bias toward action is essential to move the mission forward, so it's a skill that needs to be evidenced in next-generation leaders. Sound planning has to be undertaken, of course. But at some point the planning needs to end and the plan needs to be worked. Decisions need to be made and action taken.

Every year we do our company planning in the third and fourth quarters. We make a couple passes at it, and then we approve it sometime in November or December. We could spend more time trying to get the plan precise, but I've learned over the years that the extra tweaking isn't worth the time involved. The plan is simply that…a plan. It gives direction but isn't set in stone. Invariably we have a variance from the plan in January or February because circumstances beyond our control ensure we can never emulate the plan exactly.

Julie and I employ this same process each year when it

comes to our personal budgeting. We set a plan between Christmas and New Year's Day for the following year. Then we start acting on it.

Encourage Your Employees to Grow

These characteristics in next-generation leaders don't magically appear. They're characteristics that are thought about and looked for by company management, beginning with the interviewing and hiring process. They are kept in the forefront of a manager's thinking as the employees are encouraged to develop them and grow over their years with the organization.

One of the strengths of a great leader is the ability to hire potential leaders with the characteristics highlighted in this chapter. As you look around your organization, what do you see? Do you think about each person you hire as a potential building block on which the future of your organization might depend? Do you have a potential successor?

8

FOLLOW WELL TO LEAD WELL

Key Actions of a Successor

A young man once told me that while he knew he had all the skills to become a solid leader, he didn't seem able to make headway in his leadership goals even after several years of trying. The promotions he'd expected didn't happen, nor did they seem to be forthcoming. We talked for a while and as we did it became obvious that for all his efforts, he hadn't learned one of the most important principles in leadership: *To lead well, you must first follow well.*

Followers aren't people merely attracted to the mission of the enterprise. Followers anticipate where the boss is going and work to get there one step ahead of him or her. Great followers realize they are stewards of their positions, and it's their job to focus on making the business—and the boss—successful. They understand the importance of knowing the will of the boss and acting accordingly. They know that power, prerogatives, and authority are resident in the boss. They realize their work is about the boss and where he wants the company to go.

When I first came to Ronald Blue & Co. I wasn't a good follower. As you recall, I was bent on eventually becoming the leader and being in charge. I had no clue about the principles

I'm going to share in this chapter. I thought it was Ron's job to make me happy. The idea of me helping *him* reach his goals and be successful was the furthest thing from my mind.

When you learn the principles of "followership" and apply them, you will immediately notice a shift in the way you work and the way your manager responds to you. You will act and respond with a greater sense of purpose and motivation. This will not only help your company move forward, but it also will help you move up in the organization.

Becoming an Excellent Follower

So what does it take to become an excellent follower? Though not exhaustive, here are some of my observations. First, we must realize that each one of us is *called to follow the person of Jesus*. The calling of the first disciples demonstrates this:

> As Jesus was walking beside the Sea of Galilee, he saw two brothers, Simon called Peter and his brother Andrew. They were casting a net into the lake, for they were fishermen. "Come, follow me," Jesus said, "and I will send you out to fish for people." At once they left their nets and followed him (Matthew 4:18-20).

Following God means that our minds and hearts are set on His interests and purposes, not our own or those of other men and women. Peter is an illustration of how a person can get a wrong focus. He believed he loved Jesus and was following Him, but we see him at one point getting totally off track. When Peter rebuked Jesus for speaking plainly about the suffering that was to come, the disciple's mind wasn't set on the things of God. Jesus firmly pointed that out to him. In fact, the Savior was quite blunt:

> When Jesus turned and looked at his disciples, he rebuked Peter. "Get behind me, Satan!" he said. "You do not have in mind the concerns of God, but merely human concerns" (Mark 8:33).

Second, great followers seek to *stay one step ahead of their boss*. They learn to anticipate where the boss is going and are aware of the boss' expectations. Great followers know what needs to be done, and they do it without input from the boss. And because they are such good students of the boss, they know what to do almost instinctively. Several of my key next-generation leaders are great at this. When they meet with me, they come with memos with answers already spelled out in anticipation of what they believe I'll ask about. Many times my assistant has already made an appointment or scheduled something without me having to ask. The more they get there ahead of me, the more I trust them. The more autonomy they have, the more freedom we all experience. This is a win for my followers and me.

This trait of "Anticipatory Followership" is one of the quickest paths to more responsibility and subsequent leadership. Why? The more you can take off of your boss' plate, the more discretionary time he or she has. The more proactive you as follower become, the more value you bring to the entity or business.

Third, terrific followers *exceed expectations*. Not only do great followers get to the goal one step ahead of the boss, they do their work thoroughly, accurately, and beyond what was expected. This exemplary work is evidence of going above and beyond, which gives the boss more confidence in the followers, resulting in more responsibility being delegated to them. The followers become more and more vital to the success of the business.

Several years ago I decided to move the field leaders' reporting to one of my followers. It was a tough decision to make. However, as this individual took charge of the role, he implemented monthly calls and other processes that resulted in more being accomplished than when I was leading the group. Each year as I observed this man's initiative, my confidence in his ability to lead grew. As a result, I've given him more and more freedom, as well as increasing responsibility. His leadership responsibilities within the company are expanding due to his exemplary work on the tasks I gave him.

Fourth, *make your leader look good*. This is a key trait of great followers. I was horrible at this early in my career because I thought my work was all about me. I sought to create my own position and gain the accolades for myself. That is never a good idea. When you try to elevate yourself, you will be humbled. When you humble yourself, you will be elevated. King Solomon wrote, "He who tends the fig tree will eat its fruit, and he who cares for his master will be honored" (Proverbs 27:18 NASB). Luke spelled this principle out even more:

> When you are invited by someone to a wedding feast, do not take the place of honor, for someone more distinguished than you may have been

invited by him, and he who invited you both will come and say to you, "Give your place to this man," and then in disgrace you proceed to occupy the last place. But when you are invited, go and recline at the last place, so that when the one who has invited you comes, he may say to you, "Friend, move up higher"; then you will have honor in the sight of all who are at the table with you. For everyone who exalts himself will be humbled, and he who humbles himself will be exalted (Luke 14:8-11 NASB).

I didn't realize that the very thing I wanted (to be elevated to leadership) would only happen as I *followed and supported* Ron with a heart bent toward making him look good. As I took on the tasks he didn't enjoy or wasn't gifted in without asking for credit, and, in fact, allowing him the credit, I was actually advancing toward my goal of being promoted to leadership. However, when I tried to take credit for my actions or ignored Ron's dreams, desires, and goals in pursuit of what I wanted, I was short-circuiting my career aspirations. Jimmy Collins, in his book *Creative Followership*, put it this way: "Let others see the boss in you."[1]

Fifth, always *build a relationship with the leader*. In the early years of my career I really underestimated how critical this was. I didn't work to have a relationship with Ron. I felt as long as I produced and accomplished the results he wanted, I would be okay. In my mind it was up to him to reach out to me. The problem with this line of thinking is that it undermined my ability to support Ron and help him succeed. Since I wasn't tuned in to him and didn't have a strong relationship with him, I didn't know much about his dreams and aspirations. That meant I definitely couldn't get there one step ahead of him.

Relationships are critical for followers to master if they ever want to follow well and, thus, eventually lead well. I'm convinced my demotion was primarily the result of my failure in this area. Now as a leader I can see why. No leader wants followers who aren't really taking their concerns and issues to heart. A leader doesn't want to spend his or her energy wondering what the followers are up to. A leader wants to ask, "Are they with me or not?" And he or she wants to know the answer is, "They are with me!"

Influence Grows as You Follow Well

As you follow well, the very thing you want (having more impact in the organization) is realized. When you do the things just mentioned, you grow in influence within the entire organization. Developing influence is a huge part of becoming a strong leader. *Influence* is a function of competence, authority, personality, character, experience, maturity, trustworthiness, and interpersonal skills. It also includes ethically using authority. In no way does it include schmoozing a leader. Most of us know what that looks like, and it's not true influence. *Influence that makes a difference* includes the right measure of judgment along with knowing how to advise the leader (or leadership teams) on strategic ideas and plans.

As a great follower, you want to leverage your influence to help your company or organization grow and succeed. To do this, you need to produce results and demonstrate good judgment. A lot of people miss this very important step in the leadership journey because they're only thinking about their own advancement plans. Let's look at some actions necessary to become a person of great influence.

Don't Go Around Your Boss

When followers fail to build a relationship with their leader so he or she can become interested in and open to their ideas, they lose influence. If followers try to take credit instead of letting the leader implement the ideas without acknowledging the source, they lose influence. "Water cooler talks" with anyone other than your boss in an attempt to gain credit for an action instead of allowing the leader leeway to use the idea is a sure way to lose influence and subsequent leadership opportunities. I know this firsthand. I worked to get the credit, not to help make Ron successful. If I had an idea, instead of allowing the idea to flow through him as I should have, I tried to keep the credit for myself. Not a good career plan.

Be Patient—Ideas Take Time to Implement

In the early days of my career, I wanted everything to happen immediately. Any idea I had, especially when I thought it was a good one, should be implemented posthaste. I've learned over the years, however, that greater wisdom comes when I'm patient and willing to allow the time necessary for others to embrace my ideas. Recognizing that change takes place slowly keeps me from coming across as too demanding and forceful, which can derail the process of influencing others to get on board. When I slowed down, I had more time to think and listen to the people around me. This also allowed me to show my care for those who were working with me. This pace change allowed me to gradually grow in influence.

Today when I meet with young leaders who haven't yet learned this lesson, I smile as they struggle to slow down. I've been there. I encourage them that even though they may have good ideas and in most cases are right, if they move too fast they will lose influence—the very thing they want most to attain.

Influence Requires More Than Productivity

Years ago I falsely believed that results were all that mattered. Since I was producing, in my mind I thought everyone should embrace my ideas. After all, they could see by the results that my ideas were working. It took several years for me to understand that even if I had a good idea and I was right on an issue, if I didn't take the time to balance my knowledge with the insights and wisdom of others so they'd join me, I couldn't bring my influence to bear in a positive manner.

Although production and results can get you on the playing field of influence, it's not enough in and of itself. Relational equity, global thinking, and political savvy to navigate company politics are also necessary to develop the influence needed to become an effective leader.

Never Murmur About Bad Decisions

When your leader makes a bad decision, don't murmur about it. Not only will this break the level of trust you're working to achieve, but it may also hamstring your influence with your boss. At some point every boss makes a bad decision. This happens because the area of decision making is always bigger than the area of knowledge. No one ever says, "Hey, I think I'll make a bad decision today." Bad decisions occur due to imperfect processes, imperfect people, and incomplete information. This is where you step in as a helpful follower.

When you provide the necessary information for the boss to make better decisions, your level of influence soars with him or her. As the company does better due to your help, you grow more in influence. You will likely find that the leadership of the company will turn to you more often because you've learned the key to influence. You've discovered influence isn't about personal power but rather about your willingness to come alongside to help and support those in leadership. This is what I appreciate so much about my executive team. They are thinking…and thinking well…so that I can continue to look forward and focus on new ideas for the business.

Stop Thinking You're Always Right

Believing you're always right is a result of pride, and it can stop your influence cold. Early in my career I was told by a mentor, "Russ, you can be right and be dead wrong." What did that comment mean? It meant that even if I were right, if I didn't learn how to positively influence people to implement the change or idea I had, then it was of no use to the company or to me.

I also needed to learn that I wasn't the only one with good ideas. Others had them too, and allowing them their day in the sun on certain issues was okay. I didn't always have to be right; I didn't always have to get my way. Allowing others to see their ideas come to fruition and giving them credit along the way, rather than diminishing my influence actually allowed my influence to increase. To grow in influence, I had to remove "I" from my vocabulary and replace it with "us" and "we."

Refuse to Practice Bad Politics

Politics is the practice of interpersonal skills. Clean politics can bring influence to bear through *covenantal behavior* and skillful observance of the processes and principles upon which the entity operates. In other words, everyone plays by the rules. Clean politics has its motivation rooted in the right heart intentions. It means playing by the rules. The focus of clean politics is to promote the entity and mission, not the individual.

Bad politics is noncovenantal and evidenced by many of the things great followers avoid, such as going behind a person's back and murmuring. It's trying to make others look bad so we look good. Bad politics is cutting and divisive.

Here are two important hallmarks for practicing good politics:

- *Great followers ask questions.* Those with the most influence are always asking questions to better understand what's going on in the entity or business. A broader understanding of the nuances of the entity allows for more insightful input and influence.

- *Great followers work to be heard.* The best followers join committees and show their ability to make good decisions even if they have a limited sphere of influence at the time. They look for ways to bring value to the business.

So many people today clamor to be noticed and get ahead. My challenge to you is found in 1 Peter 5:6, which contains a powerful truth about leadership. Practice it and you will see your influence soar. "Humble yourselves, therefore, under God's mighty hand, that he may lift you up in due time."

Dealing with Bad Leadership

I want to drop in a note about working under bad leadership. Not every boss receives rave reviews. In fact, there will be some who will make you wonder how in the world they're still working within the organization. They exhibit none of the traits discussed in this book. A bad boss or incompetent leader *is not* an acceptable excuse for failure in followership. Unless there is immoral or illegal behavior occurring, good followers need to learn how to go about their business in the right way. So what are you as a follower to do under poor leadership? You only have two choices: either stay and get on board by following the leader or leave. As Jimmy Collins put it, "Either get on board and support the boss or fire him. Yes, that's right. One of the options is to fire the boss!"[2] Obviously by "firing the boss" he means making the choice to leave, which certainly is a valid option.

So what's the best way to process this decision? First, if there's nothing unethical that would require you to leave, ask: "Is there something I can learn in this difficult situation?" After facing what amounted to a significant demotion in the mid-90s,

I wondered if I needed to leave the firm. I realized that doing so at that point in my life wouldn't be a wise decision. I couldn't find God's peace about bolting. I sensed I needed to allow God to work in my life and that He had me in this time of testing for a reason.

It's my experience that for most people the vocational environment is a prime training ground God uses to teach us and make us more usable. Far too often people miss these prime opportunities to grow by leaving difficult environments too quickly. I'm not saying you should never make the choice to leave, but often the trials you face when dealing with difficult bosses are the very things God uses to shape you for your next position. Looking back, I realize it was necessary for me to be brought down so that I'd stop thinking that "being boss was all about me" and start listening to what God wanted me to hear.

If you feel you do need to leave a company or situation due to bad leadership, I advise you to take time to seek God's direction. Allow Him to prompt you and move you in the direction He wants you to go. I also encourage you to open up your thinking to the possibility that God may leave you right where you are so He can train you and enrich your life with faith and the truth of His principles. Paul admonished Timothy on several occasions to "stand firm" in his faith. Many times it takes more discipline and courage to stand firm in a test than it does to turn and run. Choosing to leave before learning what God wants you to learn only means you'll likely go somewhere else and start the process all over again. Basically, until you deal with *your* issues, you'll take them with you to the next assignment.

If you feel like you've learned what you need to learn in

your current situation and you've done all you can to follow and make your boss a success but it's just not working out, then "fire your boss" as Collins recommends. It's not healthy for you, your boss, or the entity for you to stay if you can't follow wholeheartedly.

If you decide to stay in an organization where the leadership is difficult for you to deal with, make sure you wholeheartedly support the vision and mission of the company despite the difficulties. You can have a bad leader but still believe in and support the mission of the enterprise. If you choose to stay, commit yourself to implementing the actions we discussed earlier. In addition, since you have a difficult boss, pay special attention to these actions:

- Be positive and not negative around others.

- Resolve any conflict as quickly as possible.

- Continue to treat those in leadership with dignity and respect.

During the years that I was chief operations officer (COO) of the firm, I lost influence because I wasn't practicing the principles of good followership. Instead, my work world operated around my ability to produce results; thus, I was focused on me and not others. The biggest lessons I learned during my ten years in the wilderness were to work on my relationships, be a better communicator, improve at business politics, let others get the credit, and stop being negative. Once I was finally able to absorb these critical lessons, my career trajectory changed for the better.

Followers who grow in influence are priceless in any organization. Every entity is changing, and no leader can know everything about everything. They must depend on their followers to help them avoid wrong turns along the way. When you think about it, a position of influence may be more impactful than a position of leadership.

9

FREEDOM FROM FOLLOWING

Gaining What You Want

Following is not a passive activity. It involves a transformation from lagging behind or not being up to speed to moving ahead and anticipating what's next. One of my greatest desires is to give our employees solid opportunities to become all that God created them to be. I want them to be fulfilled in their work and have as much freedom as possible. In this chapter we'll consider two forms of freedom that come from following. First is freedom in your day-to-day work. The second is freedom from being a follower.

Freedom in Your Day-to-Day Work

At Ronald Blue & Co. we have set a goal of helping our employees understand how to gain freedom to perform the responsibilities of their positions. It's our belief that people are most fulfilled in their jobs when they operate at a high level of autonomy. This autonomy, however, is something that has to be earned over time. As the team member becomes more and more competent in handling the work they've been given to do, they're given more freedom.

Freedom from our vantage point means employees have gained control of the *what, when,* and *how* of the work and are trusted to do it independently. They have earned the right to work autonomously by performing the various tasks responsibly and in such a way that they gained their managers' confidence and eased their managers' anxiety level. As the managers become increasingly comfortable with the employees' ability to do their jobs well, the employees are given a higher degree of freedom in the day-to-day aspects of their roles (less input and supervision from the managers).

So when does this journey to freedom typically begin? The moment the individual joins the organization. When we hire new team members, we know they have a certain skill set that we believe is a good fit for the positions we have available. However, until the employees come on board and are given actual work to do, we don't know with certainty their true capabilities.

Let's consider a real example in our firm. When we hire financial planners, we expect them to be able to perform certain tactical aspects of their job fairly quickly. This includes such things as being computer savvy, understanding tax laws, being proficient in reading wills and insurance policies, and other basic tasks related to financial services. Though the new employees bring a good deal of knowledge to the job, they haven't yet learned how Ronald Blue & Co. does financial planning. We certainly wouldn't ask or expect them to be able to prepare a financial plan to our specifications on day one.

Instead, they work with their manager, explaining what they're planning to do *before* they actually prepare their first plan. By running their thinking by their manager in advance, they can be sure they're on the right track. This type of interaction early on gives the employees the opportunity to learn how to do things the way we want them done and to gain insights into their manager's expectations. The employees would act on the plan only after getting the okay from the manager to move forward. While the team member has control of *what* goes into his or her work output at this stage, the manager governs the *timing* of the work until the content meets our company's standards.

If we've hired well, we don't expect the planners to remain at this beginning stage for long. As the planners show the ability to prepare plans accurately with minimal or no additional input from the manager, they earn the manager's confidence and trust. They are then allowed to work more independently with no advance consultation required. The planners are able to do the work on their own time schedule, letting the manager know when the work is complete. Now the planners control the *content* and the *timing*.

As the planners continue to show good thinking skills and the ability to produce accurate, high-quality work, they gain more and more autonomy, eventually earning the right to prepare financial plans independently on a day-in and day-out basis. Manager advice and approval on the front end and even on the back end are no longer needed. The team members have learned what needs to be done and how to do it. The manager is confident they know what to do and how to do it, so the employees are given the freedom to do the job. At this point, the manager has confidence in the competence of the planners and has given them total freedom to make decisions on the *what*, *when*, and *how* of the work. They have earned the right to do the next plan with no input from the manager.

Now, I'd like you to step back and look at this for a moment. Do you see what has happened at this point? Not only have the planners gained freedom, but so has the manager. Less management time is required because the planners are equipped and engaged in doing the work. This allows the manager to focus on other things. The manager is able to accomplish more, and production goes up because of the confidence earned by the followers (the planners in our case). The manager has more success, the company grows, and the planners become more and more vital to the company. Over time, the manager hands off more of the work to the planners, and the planners are more empowered, experiencing a greater degree of satisfaction in their work.

I joined Ronald Blue & Co. in much the same way. At first I had limited freedom with significant oversight. The fact that I came from a teaching background meant I had much to learn in the financial services arena. As a newbie, I had a little bit of influence over what went into my work, but I was given no control over timing. I was told what things I needed to do, given deadlines to meet, and then told what follow-up items needed to be handled. I quickly realized that if I wanted to have more autonomy and control over my work environment, I needed to produce, earn Ron's confidence, and discover how to stay one step ahead of him. If he had a meeting coming up, rather than waiting for him to tell me what to do, I tried to anticipate what he would need to be prepared for the meeting, and I'd get that work done accordingly. This subsequently led to increased freedom for me.

All leaders want competent followers who will help make their jobs easier, giving them more freedom to focus on other things. If you're currently serving in a follower role, you can earn more freedom by helping your manager have...

- *confidence in your competence* by producing exceptional results on a consistent basis

- *respect for your character* by demonstrating a high level of integrity daily

- *rapport with your personality* by making an effort to connect or build a relationship with him or her

Now, let's take a moment to look at the flip side of this equation. What managers do *not* want are followers they can't depend on. Managers don't want to worry or be nervous about the assignments they've given out. What do I mean by this? Let's go back to our planners example. If a planner prepares a plan but makes some incorrect assumptions, doesn't get the job done on time, or is missing key information that was accessible, this would cause the manager anxiety and make him or her wonder, "What else might not be up to par here?"

When an employee is new, this might happen once or twice, but if it continues, the planner would likely be more closely supervised until he or she gains the manager's confidence. For a time, the planner will be expected to keep the manager informed of the progress of the work and, perhaps, be required to check everything with the manager before proceeding to the next step. In this situation, the planner has lost control of the *how*, *what*, and *when* of the work, and the manager has to spend more time checking to see what's been done and whether it's been done correctly. This is a lose-lose situation that doesn't lead to satisfaction or success for either person.

Other examples of behaviors great followers *avoid* include:

- telling the manager about problems without proffering solutions

- continually waiting to be told what to do

- plopping problems on the manager's desk for him or her to handle

In my career there have been a few times when team members came to me with problems and no solutions were offered. Their problems were now my problems. Needless to say, this was not a good move for anyone. I'm thinking, *Why can't they take care of this situation? Why aren't they thinking about potential solutions? What do they want me to do with it?* Because this was their job to handle, and I already had plenty to do, they put more work on my plate instead of taking work off. I gradually became less receptive to ideas they proffered. They lost my confidence and, as a result, I became less open to what they had to say. They lost value and freedom in the organization.

That is the opposite of what any leader wants from followers. The more followers stay out in front of their manager by solving problems, offering recommendations, evidencing good thinking and insight, and producing good results, the more freedom and autonomy they experience in their day-to-day work.

If you're currently serving in a follower role, I want to caution you that a couple words you never want to hear your manager say are *nervous* and *anxious*. At Ronald Blue & Co. we help our new employees understand that their jobs are to make sure their manager isn't worried about anything they're doing. Their goal is to help the manager have *confidence in their competence* as quickly as possible. This requires them to learn what the manager needs and how he or she likes to receive information. Obviously every job has many components, and you may gain autonomy in some but not all of what you do for a period of time. Even so, your goal should be to gain autonomy in the majority of what you do and to help your manager have increasing confidence in your ability to get the job done even as you continue to learn and grow.

If you're currently serving in a leadership role, you too need to understand this confidence/anxiety dynamic in order to provide clarity to your team members. It's important for you to effectively articulate what you need from your team members so they can improve their ability to meet your needs and earn the opportunity to work independently. This shouldn't be a guessing game for those who are trying to follow you. This requires you to have an understanding of what will help you feel comfortable when they have the ball, as well as having a willingness to share this information. It's your responsibility to help your team members know where they stand freedom-wise. It should be the aim of the team members to understand what you need, deliver what you need, and do their work with excellence as they strive to get to the main goal a step ahead of you.

Freedom from Being a Follower

"Freedom from following" is the second benefit that occurs

as you gain autonomy. Not only does your work environment become more free and fulfilling, but you will also find yourself growing into a leadership position with people following you. Before going further, I want to mention that you will never be completely free from following someone. Even as CEO I follow our Management Committee's recommendations. I report to them and need to stay one step ahead of them if I expect to remain in my role. In churches the senior pastor has an elder board, and a Fortune 500 company has a board of directors. With any well-run entity, there's someone even the leader must follow. Total freedom and autonomy from following will never exist. And as disciples of Jesus Christ, we're called to be His followers all the time.

What I mean by "freedom from being a follower" is that you develop more opportunities to act independently. The majority of your job description allows you autonomy to control the timing and content of your work. There are fewer aspects of your job that you are doing for someone else to whom you must report.

For example, I'm responsible to develop and execute a firm-wide operating plan each year that is approved by the Management Committee. Once approved, I have a good deal of autonomy and freedom in decision making about the execution of the plan. I can act independently most of the time. I can execute and decide among the various alternatives without needing someone else's approval. Very rarely do I need to go to the Management Committee for their approval on decisions related to the operating plan.

Having this level of freedom gives me a wonderful feeling of empowerment. It's my belief that we all like to feel empowered. When we own the right to make decisions, it provides significance to our work and is a key component of job satisfaction.

Since I've earned the confidence of the Management Committee during the past decade, I've been given more and more freedom and areas of responsibility that I am able to act on independently. I find this tremendously rewarding. I've also focused on building a team of strong followers, which has given me more discretionary time—one of the ultimate freedoms that come to leaders who have followed well themselves.

As a leader, you'll find that the practice of great followership will make life easier over time and ultimately make your work more fun and enjoyable. This is what I've experienced. I've found that the very thing I wanted so desperately more than two decades ago was only possible when I was willing to humble myself and learn to follow well.

10

Coaching to Build Succession
Providing Intentional Development

Hopefully by now I've convinced you that to succeed as a great leader, you must have a successor. We've spent a good deal of time talking about the reasons it's important to pour yourself into the next generation: specifically how your entity's mission is not about you and the importance of setting aside your ego to effectively serve and develop people who will carry your organization's mission into the future. We've also discussed the character traits, qualities, and behaviors that are critical in identifying next-generation leaders.

What we haven't yet talked about is the *how*. *How* do you do this? *How* do you go about *intentionally developing* those who will be the future leaders of your organization? *Where* do you even begin? *What* do you need to do to be sure those you choose to lead will be well equipped and ready for the challenge?

The next two chapters will focus on these questions to help you put into practice the things we've been talking about. In this chapter, we'll primarily look at one-on-one people development, while in the next chapter we'll look at ways to impart a more global way of thinking to your next-generation leaders.

The goal of these chapters is to provide you with practical steps you can take to begin to intentionally equip your future leaders.

Be a Coach!

I'm convinced that the best leaders are coaches at heart. I love this quote from the late Dallas Cowboys coach Tom Landry: "A coach is someone who *tells you what you don't want to hear* and has you *see what you don't want to see*, so that *you can be who you've always known you could be*." Coach Landry was clearly a leader who was committed to bringing out the best in those he led.

Effective coaches not only know how to select highly skilled players, but they also know how to develop them to reach their unrealized potential. Coaches are aware that a winning team is made up of highly effective members functioning at peak performance. Great coaches know each team member has different development needs, so they tailor their coaching to fit the needs of the individuals. They spend one-on-one time with each person on the team to help him or her learn new skills, unlearn bad habits, and then practice, practice, and practice some more. They know repetition is necessary to perfect the skills of each individual member in order for the team to be successful. They also know a team is better than highly skilled individuals operating on their own. Good coaches employ a variety of tools on a daily basis as they build their team.

What practices do effective coaches employ as they seek to build winning teams? One thing they *don't* do is tell the team members to "figure it out on their own." A good coach is hands-on and intimately involved with each team member. Daniel

Harkavy, in *Becoming a Coaching Leader*, mentions five specific techniques we'll focus on (though there are certainly more): counseling, teaching, training, consulting, and mentoring.[1]

Coach as Counselor

Counselors typically provide advice for a living. They are keen observers of behavior, paying particular attention to those that could be problematic to the counselee in the future. Counselors help people confront their issues and challenge them to think through different approaches they can take as they go forward. Counselors are often called upon to help clients deal with past problems knowing that in order for the clients to grow they may need help to overcome something from the past.

In your role of "coach counselor," this could entail helping an individual figure out how to unlearn an unproductive habit that's been holding him or her back from advancing. In our company, after sitting in on client prospect meetings with young advisors, I've counseled many of them to listen more than they talk. They're typically so excited to share all that we as a company can do to help clients they forget to listen. Listening, however, is a key to consultative selling. So after the meetings, I usually take them aside to debrief them and give them pointers.

As you observe potential leaders in your organization, you'll know where they need counsel to improve skills or eliminate the behaviors that are holding them back from advancement.

Coach as Teacher

Teachers primarily help people *understand the facts*. They show individuals how to do certain tasks. Teachers impart specific information about a given subject. Their job is to share knowledge. In your role of "coach teacher," this could involve such things as teaching an individual how to read the key reports used for decision making, showing them techniques for developing new business, or sharing a skill you know they'll need to continue to grow in the business.

In our business, I've spent much time teaching our young advisors how to conduct a "family conference," a key tool our company uses. I've shared with them the information they need to provide this service, the resources to use, when to use them, and how to facilitate the conference. I've also taught them how to lead their teams, when to have team meetings, what to do in the meetings, and so forth.

I hope you see that as a coach teacher you have knowledge to pass on! You've learned a lot through the years. Remember, what you know is not proprietary. Paul wrote, "What do you have that you did not receive?" (1 Corinthians 4:7). Be quick to offer your insights and knowledge. Share the knowledge God has entrusted to you.

Coach as Trainer

The role of a trainer is threefold: to *teach* new behaviors and skills, to *reinforce* the new behaviors when observed, and to *encourage* the learner to practice the new behaviors and skills (along with the old skills) until they're mastered. The "coach trainer" needs to be clear about what needs to be developed and help employees stay laser-focused on their skills and behaviors until they're mastered.

Think about personal fitness trainers at a local gym. What

are they doing? They're standing over the trainees making sure what they're doing is being done correctly and exhorting them to keep doing it over and over. Repetition is required to master something. Malcolm Gladwell, in his book *Outliers*, explains with detailed illustrations that to become an expert at anything requires 10,000 hours of practice.[2] If you think about it, you as the leader have probably done what you're doing at least that many hours. That's why you're the leader. In your role of coach trainer, you need to see to it that the next-generation leaders get more and more repetitions under their belts so they can become experts as well, thus preparing them to lead and be potential successors.

Let me give you an illustration of training. Let's say you have a few people who are potential successors, but they lack the necessary public speaking skills your organization requires. In addition to encouraging them to practice their skills and giving them more opportunities within the organization to do so, you may also recommend involvement with Toastmasters and other forums that will afford them opportunities to speak publicly and master this key leadership skill.

Coach as Consultant

Consultants make *specific recommendations* based on what they've observed. They typically lay out a clear course of action for others to follow. In your role of "coach consultant," you might say something like, "I noticed that when you used the national economy illustration in your talk people started to lose interest. Next time you might want to try using an example based on an individual's budget."

Whereas counselors look at the past and give input, consultants look at the present and give pointed and direct feedback to address a specific issue. Ronald Blue & Co. is a financial consulting business. As a result, we're constantly giving direct feedback to clients, such as changing insurance, making a specific investment, implementing a tax-saving technique, and so on. In my early years in the company, Ron "consulted" me on my wardrobe. He made specific recommendations about what to wear to be successful in the financial services industry. Consider your specific organization and the areas that you might act as a consultant to help your potential leaders succeed.

Coach as Mentor

Basically, mentors share their personal experiences, give advice or guidance, and provide people with insights about what has worked for them in the past. In your role of "coach mentor," you're serving as an experienced and trusted advisor. Being a mentor requires a willingness to be vulnerable in a way in which you might not be accustomed. The best mentors willingly share the things they've learned from prior successes *and* the ways they've grown and learned from past failures.

I've found that my willingness to open up and share my experiences, both good and bad, allows me to effectively build knowledge into those coming after me. They realize I'm being authentic so they are more teachable than they might be if I were standoffish or acted invincible.

Are You Willing?

While these five techniques are important to be an effective coach, they don't really tell the whole story. All are focused on helping individuals acquire the skills and knowledge levels of the coach sharing the information. But a coach's role transcends all of these because his or her focus is on helping people become the very best they can be—and this could far exceed anything the coach is personally able to do. As a coach, my hope and inspiration is to help others become all God has in store for them. My desire is to help others accomplish things they didn't even realize they were capable of.

Are you willing to be a coach? Are you willing to pour your life into those you lead so that they might improve and reach their maximum potential?

Adjusting Your Style

Just as coaches don't use a "one size fits all" approach with their team members, neither should effective leaders expect that a singular way of leading or interacting will effectively bring out the unrealized potential in all the employees for whom they've been given responsibility. Admittedly, facilitating growth will be easier to do with some people. When leading individuals who are wired similarly to the way you're wired, this development stuff is easy. You already know how they think, what they need, how they're likely to respond to your input, so you coach them like you would like to be coached. But your stewardship responsibility doesn't extend to just these few.

Well-rounded leadership teams *need* individuals with differing perspectives, viewpoints, life experiences, and ways of thinking. It's highly likely that your potential leadership pool has a lot of different folks with unique personalities, temperaments, wiring, and backgrounds. They are male and female. They come from differing environments. They have varying educational and life experiences that have helped shape who they are. Scripture says we are "fearfully and wonderfully made" (Psalm 139:14), clearly demonstrating that we're not all the same. The fact that some people are easier for you to relate to than others doesn't relieve you of your responsibility to develop the potential of *all* those you've been called to lead. Developing some of your potential future leaders might even require you to adjust your natural style (aka exercising some of your own emotional intelligence) to effectively coach them.

Think for a moment about the leadership style of Jesus. Scripture provides us with many examples that demonstrate how He adjusted His approach so that it was tailored to meet the needs of the specific individual with whom He was interacting. Take Peter, for example. Peter was a "Fire! Aim! Ready!" kind of guy. Effectively developing Peter required Jesus to take a very direct approach. Who else required a rebuke as blunt and to the point as the one Peter received: "Jesus turned and said to Peter, 'Get behind me, Satan! You are a stumbling block to me; you do not have in mind the concerns of God, but merely human concerns'" (Matthew 16:23)?

Now think about the different way Jesus gave feedback to Martha as He chided her in her own home, letting her know her thinking was off. To her He said, "Martha, Martha…you are worried and upset about many things, but few things are needed—or indeed only one. Mary has chosen what is better, and it will not be taken away from her" (Luke 10:41). And what about Paul? He was blinded while on the road to Damascus to get his attention (Acts 9:3-9). Clearly, one style doesn't fit all. Effectively leading and developing people requires a willingness and capability to adjust your leadership style to meet the needs of the individuals. A good coach knows some players respond to firm instruction, some need to see the overall game plan, while still others need an abundance of encouragement.

Great Leaders Care

In order to adjust your style to facilitate the development of all who demonstrate leadership potential in your organization, you need to truly care about them. *Care* means "to support and protect; to be attentive; to have watchful regard for." As a leader, you need to really understand your followers:

- How has God made them?
- What are their interests beyond those you see on a day-to-day basis?
- What makes them tick?
- What are their natural talents and gifts?
- What are the things that jazz them?
- What frustrates them?
- What are their ambitions?
- What do they view as their failings?
- Where do they see opportunities for growth? Are their observations consistent with what you see?

How well do you actually *know* your employees and future leaders? When was the last time you asked them what they need from you as their leader? Do you show them that you care about them and for them? Do you care enough to invest in their growth and development—even when it's difficult or inconvenient? I encourage you to continually ask yourself this question: How can you as leader create conditions that will allow employees to develop the skills and confidence needed to do their jobs to the best of their abilities? Are you committed to helping them do more than they think possible?

The Power of Questions

One of the most important skills I encourage you to develop as you embark on this coaching journey are your questioning skills. Good questions can be one of the most powerful tools in your "people development" tool kit. By questioning carefully, you can gain insights into an individual's thinking relative to his or her job, areas of responsibility, and understanding of the organization as a whole.

The answers given will help you better understand how they think, reveal areas where knowledge gaps exist, and highlight topics where additional teaching, counseling, training, consulting, or mentoring might be needed. In addition, timely and pertinent questions can be used to help your team members learn to discern appropriate courses of action, which is precisely what you want to see being developed in your next-generation leaders.

Here are a few phrases I suggest you use often:

- What do you think?
- Why don't you make that decision?

- How would you handle…?

- Will you help me understand…?

- How would you tackle that problem?

- If you were in my place, what would you do?

- What things do you think need to be considered in making that decision?

Giving your team members the answers may seem easier in the short run, but the near-term shouldn't be your focus. Good questions can facilitate the development of good thinking skills, which are critical to the success of your future leaders and your company.

Remember, the less *you* do, the more you will accomplish; the less *you* do, the more you allow *others* to accomplish. Good questions can help you make this shift.

Barriers You'll Face

Be forewarned! As you shift your focus toward more intentional people development, you need to brace yourself because you *will* be tested. Discipline will be required to keep you from drifting back into your old ways of doing things. There will always be demands for your time and attention. Are you willing to protect the time you've set aside to invest in coaching your next-generation leaders, guarding it from other important things that will surely come up? Or will you view this time as optional, allowing it to be the first thing bumped when other issues arise?

When development gets hard and requires you to spend significant time training on something new, are you willing to make the investment? Or will you backslide and do it your-self because it's easier and faster? When someone you've seen as a high-potential prospect messes up—and I guarantee that will happen—will you see it as a moment for teaching, coun-seling, or mentoring? Or will you pull the responsibility back on your own shoulders? Are you willing to give feedback that's uncomfortable if it's in the best interest of the individual? Or will you back off, let the wind blow over, and deprive the next-generation leader of an opportunity to grow?

Focusing on vocational work is always easier, but if you truly believe that equipping the next generation for leadership matters, you will stay the course and develop the disciplines and systems needed to make it happen. Preparing your orga-nization so its mission is carried into the future is your most important calling as a leader.

Where Are You Today?

A good place to begin your journey into "intentional peo-ple development" may be to examine your heart and habits to get a handle on where you are currently. The following ques-tions will give you some things to think about and, hopefully, your answers will provide a foundation for developing a road-map you can follow to ensure your people development goal as a leader is accomplished.

- Do you commonly talk more about your team's successes than your own?

- Do you derive greater satisfaction from what your team has created or what you have created?

- Do you have preset, scheduled coaching sessions with each of your key team members?

- Do you have a method for coaching your team members?

- Do you have a system for following up with them when action plans are due?

- Do you regularly provide feedback?

- Are you clear on what needs to be developed in each individual?

- Do you know where the gaps are and what needs to be learned?

- Do you know the goals of your team members? Their dreams? Their stressors? Their fears?

- Do you know what truly motivates each of your people?

If you answered no to any of these questions, this will give you an idea of where to begin your intentional coaching journey. Your successor won't just materialize ready to take the reins. He or she will need to be developed through your coaching so they can learn and employ the skills you have. Coaches never win championships; *teams do*. The mission and entity are more important than you.

11

CREATING A POOL OF FUTURE LEADERS

Implementing a Leadership Development Program

Because the idea for writing this book was birthed from a conversation about a "big picture" leadership development program we designed, I feel I wouldn't be sharing the whole message on leadership from my perspective if I didn't tell you a little bit about that program. Hopefully these thoughts will spark your imagination and encourage you to think outside the box about ways you can create experiences for your next-generation leaders to help them develop a more global view of your organization.

The Journey

As Ronald Blue & Co. embarked on our intentional leadership development journey, one of the challenges we faced was figuring out how to effectively impart global thinking across the organization, especially given our company's size, network of offices, and the limited number of opportunities our potential future leaders had for exposure to firm-wide issues. In a structure such as ours, it can be easy for people to develop a narrow view unless they're challenged to think beyond what they're able to see on a day-in and day-out basis in their immediate work environment.

While a great deal has been written on the subject of experiential development, we found there wasn't much available that was suitable for our firm. Large companies like General Electric, McKesson, AT&T, and others are known for their leadership development programs. Because of their size, they have the ability to transfer people across divisions, work groups, continents, business units, and so forth to support their goals of providing the necessary exposure and experiences to develop global thinking skills in those with leadership potential. While this all sounds well and good, this type of training program really isn't practical for most mid-sized organizations, and it certainly wasn't an option for us.

In recognition of the need to foster the development of firm-wide thinking skills—and acknowledging the lack of available models we could mimic—we created our own program, which we named the "CEO Roundtable." Maybe the concepts and the structure of this program will have some applicability for you and your organization as you build your pool of potential successors.

The Program

The CEO Roundtable is an 18-month experiential leadership development program designed to help individuals demonstrating leadership potential gain a broader view of the organization as a whole. In order to participate, the team member has to have demonstrated leadership abilities within his or her current role, be nominated to the group by either the senior leader of their office or a member of the firm's senior leadership team, and be willing to commit the time and energy required to do the work involved. The group's size is limited to ten to twelve members and is comprised of men and women who serve in various roles from different offices, departments, and work groups across the company.

The key objectives of the CEO Roundtable are to:

- proactively invest in and develop team members displaying leadership potential

- impart learning and wisdom gained by the CEO and other members of the Senior Leadership Team to those demonstrating leadership traits in the firm

- facilitate a "big picture" understanding of the firm via a "discovery" process

- provide "real time" experiential learning opportunities to promote enhanced understanding of broader business issues impacting our company

- create an environment for participants to build relationships, learn from each other, and experience the synergistic impact of working together as a team

The Structure

In order to facilitate accomplishment of the objectives, we bring the team together for five 2-day, in-person sessions, each focusing on a key aspect of building a 100-year firm. Our focus areas are *leadership, client service, financials, risk management, growth*, and *building a 100-year firm*. (Your focus areas will be the things you deem important to your business.)

Each session requires the participants to complete a set of pre-work, attend the live meetings, and work on follow-up assignments that reinforce what they've learned. To help you understand what this means a bit better, I'll break it down.

Pre-Work

The *pre-work* portion is designed to prepare the participants for the topics we're going to cover in the two-day meeting. This could be something as simple as reading a book about leadership and preparing a summary to present to the group or as complex as taking an in-depth look at their "book of business," identifying where they would like to be five and ten years down the road, and developing a plan of action that will help them get there.

I encourage you to determine the key areas for success in your organization and design the pre-work around those areas. In a church setting, it might be researching what other churches are doing for their youth programs; for a manufacturing business it might be looking at how other companies develop their bids. Pre-work should be centered around the key areas of your business.

In-Person Sessions

When we're together in our in-person sessions, we spend the time delving into our business, using the participants' pre-work to launch the discussion. Sessions generally include:

- pre-work presentations where the participants share with the group what they've learned

- a "CEO Learnings" component where I share some of my experiences in the business

- interactive time with the firm's Senior Leadership Team

- teaching elements designed to introduce the group to aspects of the business they might not have experienced yet

- case studies where participants work together in smaller teams to tackle real-life business issues we're currently experiencing

- discussion questions designed to provide insight into how they're thinking and facilitate the discovery of a broader view of the business

Follow-Up Assignments

Our follow-up assignments tend to be broad, varied, and tied to real work that needs to get done. An assignment might be spending time with a personal coach to help the participant increase his or her level of self-awareness, identify potential challenge areas, or develop a plan to foster growth in a safe environment. It could be working with team members to map out a career plan for each person or consulting with the senior leader in his or her department to identify a project to get involved in that will help develop leadership skills and positively impact the department. Future leaders might also facilitate major projects that will have firm-wide impact.

Some of the assignments can be done independently, while others require the participants to work together as a team. Some are tactical in nature. Others have a legacy component—focusing on things that will impact the direction and culture of the firm for years to come.

CEO Learnings

Though the CEO Roundtable was originally designed to provide learning experiences for our next-generation leaders, the things senior management has learned from *them* through the process have been an unexpected blessing. Many of these *learnings* have resulted in the initiation of a variety of company-wide initiatives that I believe will make us stronger going forward.

For example, we realized that our biggest annual corporate-sponsored training event wasn't hitting the mark, so we decided to turn the reins over to our next-generation leaders. They now have primary responsibility for developing the agenda for this training event. Though letting go was tough to do, the results have generated the highest meeting satisfaction ratings we've ever seen. We also discovered that although I thought I was being consistent and repetitive in my communication regarding the company's vision and direction, the message wasn't being disseminated throughout the organization. In response, we've put in place an internal communication strategy designed to reinforce the vision and connect the activities we're working on to that vision. The outcome? A 15-percent year-over-year improvement in employee understanding of where we're headed.

Another unexpected and surprising revelation was that we weren't as buttoned-up in some of our processes as I thought we were. This led to the formation of an advisory group that's working to develop resources and tools that will bring greater consistency to a key area of our business. This is a multiyear initiative, so the work isn't yet done, but we believe the actions this group takes will build a stronger foundation for our company for many years to come.

The Impact

While we're still in the process of learning what the longer-term impact of the CEO Roundtable will be, thus far the feedback has been extremely strong. We've seen a higher level of engagement among the participants. Managers have commented that they feel more supported in their offices and no longer carry the burden of being the only one who is aware of and considering the "big picture" when making decisions. We have a waiting list of men and women our managers would like to have participate in future roundtables, and there's buzz about the program among team members who are still early in their careers with us. It's our hope and prayer that through the continued implementation of this program, we'll develop leaders at all levels and create a compelling work experience for those we hope to have lead our organization in the future.

Be Prepared!

I want to give one word of caution. If you're not willing to open up and share information that will broaden the next-generation leaders' exposure (for example, the company's financials), if you aren't ready to hear what the next generation has to say, and if you aren't willing to engage them in the process of helping you make company-wide decisions, you shouldn't even *think* about going down this path.

This future leaders program is designed to *expand* thinking. I can guarantee that if you've assembled the group well and are truly bringing together a team of highly talented individuals with strong leadership potential, their output will blow you away. They are going to *want* to have impact, so you need to be willing and prepared to let them act.

Are you willing to let go? Are you open to letting others lead at times?

The Bottom Line

As you can surmise, the time required to implement a program like this is significant for the session leaders and the participants. Based on the feedback to date and the things we've been able to accomplish thus far, we believe the benefits have been well worth the time and effort.

Aside from the critical tasks of casting the vision for our firm of the future and keeping the mission fire burning, I've come to believe that developing next-generation leaders for our company is one of the single most important investments of time I can make at this stage in my career. We're striving to prepare the organization for the leadership transition we know lies ahead.

12

THE SAGE

Leaving a Mark that Lasts

When I left Kansas in the fall of 1980, I thought I knew what a leader was and what a leader did. In reality, I had no clue. Now, more than three decades later, I'm confident that the principles I've shared in this book are indeed the keys to great leadership. When leaders come to realize they are indeed dispensable and won't be around forever, they recognize that the only way anyone will know they were on this planet is by the marks they leave through their families and the people who follow them in their entities.

Types of Leaders

Ernesto Poza, in his book *Family Business*, discusses six styles of exiting leaders. I've summarized them for you:

> *Monarch*: This person doesn't leave until forced out and thinks no one can replace him or her. Unfortunately far too many leaders fit in this category and, as a result, their entities struggle.
>
> *General*: This person leaves reluctantly. He or she plots a return and is hopeful the successor fails.

This way the Board or the person who removed them is proved wrong. The general really believes he or she is irreplaceable. Generals are divisive and in no way look to help successors succeed.

Inventor: This person leaves the leadership position and moves back into more vocational work, usually in another company but sometimes in the company they had been leading.

Governor: This leader ensures the successor is trained and ready before moving on. This is the type of leader we've discussed in this book. Once the successor is trained, the governor might move to a "transition czar" position.

Transition Czar: This role provides active leadership during the overlap period when the company's reins are being handed off. This could last a few weeks or months. We see this type of transition period in the United States presidency between the November elections and the newly elected president being sworn in to office in January. This type of transition provides stability and consistency to the entity.

Ambassador: Depending on the desires of the successor and the needs of the company, this leader might serve as a representative of the company for some time. Ambassadors remain involved to help others learn about the business, and they weigh in on how to manage the business.[1]

The first three styles obviously aren't the most effective for the ongoing success of an entity. These leaders tend to drag the business or organization down and usually create a lot of collateral damage along the way. The last three styles provide a better path to a successful transition to a successor, and each one is positive in its own right. They can also be implemented simultaneously.

It's been my observation that it's very rare to see the final style (ambassador) role fulfilled successfully. That's typically because most leaders don't leave well. They stay at the monarch or general level, never seeing themselves as a governor, which would qualify them for the ambassador role.

The Sage

As Ronald Blue & Co. has matured and experienced the need to have succession at the branch and corporate levels, we've introduced another word for the leaders who have retired or will retire. That word is *sage*. I love this word. The sage role may play out in a manner similar to the ambassador, but to me calling a leader *sage* is much stronger. What do I mean by the term *sage*?

Sages are wise people with sound judgment and prudence usually gained from years of experience. They've applied their knowledge in practical and successful ways, usually because they've learned from their good and bad decisions made in the past.

I believe our company will be much better off as we figure out a way to retain and leverage the wisdom our sages have gained over their twenty-five or more years in the financial services business. Who knows financial planning and client service better than these folks? Who has more business development experience? Who has seen just about everything in this industry? Who knows best how to deal with difficult employee situations? I realized what a crime it would be if we didn't have them available—as long as they are willing and capable—to mentor our younger employees. What if these folks moved out of their corner offices and down the hall to places near the next-generation leaders?

Sage roles are only possible if the transitioning leaders think like governors, transition czars, or ambassadors. To make this change requires humility and the willingness to give up some of the accoutrements of leadership. Sages are the great leaders we've been discussing in this book. Our company will be much stronger with this retained wisdom.

Think about it. What if a senior pastor of a church is willing to yield the pulpit to a younger pastor but remain available as a sounding board for advice and to answer questions? What if a CEO retires but keeps an office down the hall and mentors the next-generation leaders? Or what if a CEO retires and moves into a position on the Board? What if a dad turns the family business over to his children and remains available for information, advice, and input? What if an older doctor is available to a younger doctor to consult with on difficult cases? In each of these scenarios, as long as the leaders let go of the reins and willingly move into advisory roles, their wisdom is retained to the benefit of the entities and next generation.

I realize moving into an ambassador or sage role isn't always possible because some leadership positions and companies don't lend themselves to this role. However, I hope this idea has at least piqued your interest enough to consider it when it's applicable to you.

I'm thrilled that we've seen several of our folks move into sage roles within our company. They've passed the leadership mantle to someone coming behind them, but they are still in the building to offer their wisdom and insights when asked. The sages won't always be with us as age takes its toll on competence and the willingness to be available. Until then, I know our company is much stronger as a result of these sages still being on our team.

Final comments

I've been in my role as CEO now for almost twelve years. I know I won't remain in this position forever, so I continue to implement the principles in this book as I build a pool of potential successors. I pour knowledge and experience into them each day, knowing that one day they will take the reins and keep the mission fire of Ronald Blue & Co. burning brightly. When that time comes, I hope I've led in such a way that I will move gracefully into a sage role to be available to my successors and the next generation. I want to exit well. In addition to my family, I can't think of a better way to leave a mark after I'm gone than to see Ronald Blue & Co. continue to carry on in a robust and compelling manner.

How about you? Are you willing to consider becoming a sage when the time comes? Will you aspire to leading your company, family business, or ministry in such a way that it will still go on strong when the time comes for you to leave? That is the best mark you can leave. What will your leadership legacy be?

NOTES

Chapter 2—Out of the Dirt

1. David W. Lambert, *Oswald Chambers: An Unbribed Soul* (Ft. Washington, PA: Christian Literature Crusade, 1989).

2. Jim Collins, *How the Mighty Fall* (New York: HarperCollins, 2009).

3. Greg Salciccioli, *The Enemies of Excellence* (New York: Crossroads Publishing Company, 2011).

4. R. Scott Rodin, Notes from the Field, "Becoming a Leader of No Reputation," http://www.christianleaders.org/JRL/Fall2002/rodin.htm, accessed 3/17/14. Nouwen quote cited by Rodin from Henri Nouwen, *In the Name of Jesus* (New York: Crossroads, 1996), 17.

5. Simon Sinek, *Start with Why* (New York: Portfolio/Penguin, 2009).

6. Neil Postman, *The Disappearance of Childhood* (New York: Delacorte Press, 1982), xi.

Chapter 3—Why Me?

1. "Great Leaders of the Bible," *Discipleship Journal,* © 1982.

2. Dallas Willard, "Living in the Vision of God," http://www.dwillard.org/articles/art view.asp?artID=96, accessed 3/17/14.

3. Ibid.

4. Joel C. Rosenberg and T.E. Koshy, PhD, *The Invested Life* (Wheaton, IL: Tyndale House Publishers, Inc., 2012), 7, emphasis in original.

Chapter 5—Great Leaders vs. Bad Leaders

1. Walter Isaacson, *Steve Jobs* (New York: Simon & Schuster, 2011), http://books.simon andschuster.com/Steve-Jobs/Walter-Isaacson/9781451648539, accessed 3/19/14.

2. Frank Wren, quoted in article by Michael I. Pellegrino, *Business-to-Business Magazine,* 2007.

Chapter 6—A Road Trip Through Potholes

1. Patrick Lencioni, *The Four Obsessions of an Extraordinary Executive* (San Francisco: Jossey-Bass, 2000), 109.

Chapter 8—Follow Well to Lead Well

1. Jimmy Collins, *Creative Followership: In the Shadow of Greatness* (Decatur, GA: Looking Glass Books, 2013), 79.

2. Ibid., 27.

Chapter 10—Coaching to Build Succession

1. Daniel Harkavy, *Becoming a Coaching Leader* (Nashville: Thomas Nelson, 2007).

2. Malcolm Gladwell, *Outliers* (New York: Back Bay Books/Little, Brown and Company, 2011), ch. 2.

Chapter 12—The Sage

1. Ernesto J. Poza, *Family Business*, 3rd ed. (Mason, OH: South-Western Cengage Learning, 2009), adapted.

About Russ Crosson

 Russ Crosson is president and CEO of Ronald Blue & Co., LLC, one of the largest independent fee-only financial, investment, tax, estate, and philanthropic advisory firms in the United States. With a national network of 13 branch offices, the firm serves more than 6500 individual and business clients.

Russ graduated from Kansas State University with a bachelor's degree in mathematics and a master's in education. He and his wife, Julie, live in Georgia and are active in teaching and mentoring married couples. They are the parents of three adult sons.

More excellent financial help from Russ Crosson and Harvest House Publishers

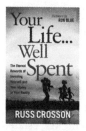

YOUR LIFE…WELL SPENT

The Eternal Rewards of Investing Yourself and Your Money in Your Family

When most Christians think about money, they think about what money can do for them right now. But attitudes about money have an eternal aspect too. Author Russ Crosson, CEO of Ronald Blue & Co. and a highly respected financial advisor, offers timely advice on how to manage money with eternity in view.

You'll discover the difference between prosperity—the accumulation of goods on this earth—and posterity—the heritage left to the generations that follow. As you explore this new way of thinking about money, about your life's work, and about how to get a higher return on life, you'll find practical suggestions for…

- developing a new understanding of work
- training up your children
- adding posterity time to busy schedules
- handling four major financial decisions
- buying vs. renting a home

www.yourlifewellspent.net

"Without the information in this book, your budget may be balanced, but unwise— your bookkeeping may be timely, but reflect only temporal values. This is the book to read first, before any others, for the renewing of your financial mind."

BRUCE WILKINSON, *The Prayer of Jabez*

THE TRUTH ABOUT MONEY LIES

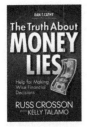

In *The Truth About Money Lies*, financial expert Russ teams up with gifted communicator Kelly Talamo to offer the truth about popular money lies that influence how you spend your money. Through stories about people like you who wrestle with spending decisions, the lies are laid bare. With truth principles based on biblical wisdom you'll discover how to counter common lies, including:

- 10 percent is God's; 90 percent is mine
- I can't afford to give
- my security is in my investments
- my talents and abilities produce my wealth
- the harder I work, the more money I make

You'll be better equipped to make informed financial decisions and use money wisely as you apply these principles for sound financial health. **www.truthaboutmoneylies.com**

8 IMPORTANT MONEY DECISIONS FOR EVERY COUPLE

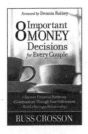

Every marriage experiences conflict. And many of those conflicts are related to finances. Russ Crosson, president and CEO of Ronald Blue & Co., shows you how to avoid the landmines caused by financial turmoil.

Russ reveals biblical wisdom regarding marriage and money and shows you how to resist defaulting to the world's view. You'll find helpful and practical advice on common areas of money management conflicts:

- men who work too much
- why wives work
- the problem of debt
- making sound investments
- giving wisely
- understanding insurance

To avoid pitfalls, Russ offers a game plan you can use to achieve harmony in your marriage regardless of your current financial situation.

RonaldBlue&Co.®

Wisdom for Wealth. *For Life.*

▶ *Corporate Profile*

Founded in 1979, Ronald Blue & Co. is one of the largest independent fee-only wealth management firms in the United States with more than $8 billion of assets under management, a network of 13 branch offices, serving more than 6,000 clients through five distinct divisions (12/31/14). The firm provides comprehensive financial strategies based on biblical wisdom designed to enrich the lives of clients across the wealth spectrum in these key areas:

- Financial, retirement, estate, and trust planning
- Investment management and solutions
- Family office services
- Philanthropic counsel and strategies
- Business consulting
- Institutional client services

▶ *Ronald Blue & Co. Branch Offices*

Ronald Blue & Co.'s financial professionals serve clients from the following office locations:

Atlanta, GA	Baltimore, MD	Charlotte, NC	Chicago, IL
Holland, MI	Houston, TX	Indianapolis, IN	Montgomery, AL
Nashville, TN	Orange County, CA	Orlando, FL	Phoenix, AZ
Seattle, WA			

▶ *Contacting Ronald Blue & Co.*

Internet: www.ronblue.com
Mail: 300 Colonial Center Parkway
Suite 300
Roswell, GA 30076

Phone: 800.841.0362
Fax: 770.280.6001
E-mail: info@ronblue.com